BY WHAT AUTHORITY?

BY WHAT AUTHORITY?

The Standards of Truth in the Early Church

by

BRUCE SHELLEY
Professor of Church History
Conservative Baptist Theological Seminary
Denver, Colorado

Wipf & Stock
PUBLISHERS
Eugene, Oregon

Wipf and Stock Publishers
199 West 8th Avenue, Suite 3
Eugene, Oregon 97401

By What Authority
The Standards of Truth in the Early Church
By Shelley, Bruce
Copyright©1965 Eerdmans
ISBN: 1-57910-187-9
Publication date 10/29/1998
Previously published by Eerdmans, 1965

To Mary,
*whose patience and sacrifice
have made life's labor
a blessed calling*

PREFACE

These are exciting days. We are witnessing challenge and conflict on every hand. Social, political, moral, and ideological battlelines are constantly shifting.

During such times of rapid change people usually tend to be preoccupied with the present. In the face, then, of so many contemporary revolutions how can we justify a volume concerned with an old, old problem? What possible relevance can the chief priests' question fired at Jesus (Matt. 21:23) have for our twentieth-century crises? A great deal indeed.

As futility thickens and despair deepens, men seem all the more inclined to believe any voice that speaks loud enough and long enough. Adolf Hitler was no nightmare. Too many graves witness to his reality. Our contemporary world itself argues that the question must be, "By what authority?"

Furthermore, if the current concern for Christian renewal is to become more than a willowy wish, it too will have to wrestle with our problem. Recent writing testifies to as much. A steady stream of articles devoted to religious authority, evangelical and liberal, popular and scholarly, pours from the presses. The World Council of Churches' doctrinal affirmation at New Delhi and the Roman Catholic document *De Ecclesia* with its statement on "Collegiality" issued by Vatican Council II indicate that religious authority is far from a dead issue.

But what century, other than the first, contributed most to a Christian pattern of authority? The second! Then let

Ignatius and Polycarp and Justin and Irenaeus be heard. We may disagree with their conclusions, but can we afford to reject them before we have understood them?

My original interest in the early Fathers' pattern of authority was aroused by Dr. George Forell, Professor of Protestant Theology at the School of Religion, State University of Iowa. I gratefully acknowledge my debt to him. Readers of the *Bulletin of the Evangelical Theological Society* will recognize Chapter VIII as a revision of an article that first appeared in the *Bulletin* with the title, "Scripture, Tradition and Authority in the Second Century." My thanks are due the editors for allowing me to use much of the material in this new form. Finally, I would like to thank Mr. William McConnell, who arranged the indexes, and Miss Elaine Potter, who prepared the typescript.

BRUCE SHELLEY

Denver Colorado

Contents

Preface		7
I	INTRODUCTION	11
II	THE EARLY SECOND CENTURY: THE APOSTOLIC FATHERS (Part I)	25
III	THE EARLY SECOND CENTURY: THE APOSTOLIC FATHERS (Part II)	41
IV	THE MID-SECOND CENTURY: THE APOLOGISTS	60
V	THE LATE SECOND CENTURY: IRENAEUS AND TERTULLIAN The Creed and the Rule of Faith	84
VI	THE LATE SECOND CENTURY: IRENAEUS AND TERTULLIAN Tradition and Scripture	100
VII	THE EARLY THIRD CENTURY: CLEMENT AND ORIGEN	126
VIII	THE SUM OF IT	139
Appendix A	THE WORK OF THE HOLY SPIRIT	152
Selected Bibliography		159
Indexes		163

I

INTRODUCTION

ONE OF CHRISTIANITY'S EARLIEST DESPISERS ONCE WROTE: "The following rules are laid down by Christians, even by the more intelligent among them. 'Let none draw near to us who is educated, or shrewd, or wise. Such qualifications are in our eyes an evil. But let the ignorant, the idiots, and the fools come to us with confidence.'"[1]

This was Celsus' way of protesting the authoritative character of Christianity. He knew all too well that the human understanding has to be captured and humbled in order to receive the Christian message. To preach the gospel is to preach with authority. If God lives, as the follower of Christ asserts, then man's existence is transformed into a destiny not of his own making. His life and liberty are suddenly circumscribed by the will of God. If Christ is to be Lord at all he must be Lord of all.

It does not follow, however, that only "the ignorant, the idiots, and the fools" can find Christ. Even Celsus knew of some "noble and mighty" who had been called. Authority in the Christian realm is spared from authoritarianism by

[1] Quoted by Origen, *Against Celsus*, III, xliv.

the mission of the Holy Spirit. The rebel in every man does not submit to a way of life alien to man. By the Spirit of God man finds the true goal of his rebellious strivings. Created in the image of God, which makes possible his rebellion, he finds fulfillment in the gospel applied to his heart by the Spirit.

Yet it remains true that any religion worthy of the name must have man's allegiance. Religion is simply authority applied to living. Theology is authority applied to thinking. Therefore no more fundamental religious question can be raised than, "By what authority?" It is antecedent to all other questions about living and thinking. This is true both logically and historically.

The Problem of Authority

It was inevitable that early Christians should meditate upon the facts that they had experienced or received as the foundation of their faith. They wished to understand them for themselves and to justify them before others. This thinking about the realities of their revelation involved theology. Christian theology is thus as old as Christianity itself.

Only with the passing of time, however, could the problem of authority as we know it arise. As long as Jesus Christ and his apostles lived, there was no clear Christian consciousness of any such problem. The source of truth was a living witness. Our problem is posed by the historical gap that exists between Christ's advent and the sources of authenticity in our own time. Here the major Christian groups divide more fundamentally than at any other point.

The Roman Catholic Church fills the gap between our Lord and contemporary Christians by the authority of the Church and what it calls its *magisterium*. This *magisterium* is the official teaching body of the Church headed by the Pope. The position is based upon the assumption that Jesus Christ transferred his authority to the apostles and their validly ordained successors, the bishops. The question of "apostolic succession" therefore looms large in the Roman Catholic scheme of authority.

Eastern Orthodoxy slightly alters the Roman pattern of authority by accenting the liturgical authority over the teach-

INTRODUCTION   13

ing authority and by stressing the early Church Councils and the Fathers over the Papacy. The doctrinal importance of the first seven ecumenical councils rests in the creeds, definitions, and canons produced. In any case, "tradition" holds a significant place in Eastern Orthodoxy as it does in Roman Catholicism.

Classical Protestantism does not question the authority that Christ conferred upon the apostles, but it asserts that the apostles were unique. Their authority as recipients of revelation cannot be handed on to others. The gap between Christ and the contemporary believer is filled by the words of the Bible and the witness of the Holy Spirit. The Bible is the once-for-all prophetic and apostolic testimony of divine revelation which the Spirit applies to believers in every generation.

It was the lot of believers in the second century to encounter this problem first. The time gap between Jesus Christ and themselves became increasingly apparent as the spread of the gospel brought the Christian message into contact with pagan thought. Ideas alien to the earliest message began to challenge the gospel. Differences of opinion cropped up, not only over minor matters but also over some doctrines striking at the life stream of the religion of the cross. For the first time Christians began to reflect upon two basic questions: What are the sources of Christian truth and how are they to be interpreted? The church's struggle with this twofold problem makes the second century one of the most important centuries in all the history of Christian thought. In this volume we hope to raise again these two questions and to see how the church constructed its earliest pattern of authority.

The Contemporary Significance

The special relevance of this problem for our time emerged with two twentieth-century events within Christendom. One of these was theological, the other organizational.

At the turn of the twentieth century Protestant liberalism was enjoying its greatest hour. While the majority of Protestant ministers in the churches were still evangelical, the seminaries, where the churches' future was being forged, fell one by one under the spell of liberalism. In the past half century all that has changed. The neat distinction between liberal and conservative no longer prevails. Modern theology has encountered a new rival.

Several factors and many names lie behind this turn of events, but if we were forced to look for the crossroads, with most churchmen we would turn toward Basel and the Swiss theologian Karl Barth. When Barth published his now famous *Commentary on Romans* in 1918, the theological movement called variously "neo-orthodoxy," "crisis theology," and "Barthianism" was born. The results of that reawakening in theology are now widely known. For our purposes it is sufficient to point out that one of the results of this "new orthodoxy" has been a renewed interest in the Bible among many Protestants. Many men trained in the liberal school began to take the Bible way of looking at things with a new seriousness. Theologians, so long preoccupied with psychology, comparative religions, and higher criticism, were driven to ask whether, after all, this really deserved the name theology. Might there be, as Barth claimed, a special revelation of God in history recorded between the covers of the Bible?

Along with this theological change a movement has emerged that has come to embrace a large segment of the Christian Church. We refer to the ecumenical movement whose modern birthday is usually considered to be the International Missionary Conference at Edinburgh in 1910. It does not fall to us to trace the history of this movement or of the World Council of Churches that resulted. It is sufficient to underscore the authority issue in all efforts toward Christian unity.

To take one example, the question of apostolic succession in Anglican and Protestant discussions regarding unity is extremely important. "I make so bold as to claim," Henri D'Espine has written in *The Ecumenical Review,* "that the doctrine of the Apostolic Succession, and the ecclesiology it implies, form the great obstacle to unification of the Church."[2]

An equally complex problem for ecumenical leaders is the nature of Biblical authority. The meeting of theologians and laymen at Oxford in the summer of 1949 was particularly

---

[2] Henri D'Espine, "The Apostolic Succession as an Ecumenical Issue," *Ecumenical Review,* IV (January, 1952), p. 159.

INTRODUCTION   15

significant in this regard. From that meeting the document *The Bible and the Church's Message* emerged. This treatise was later enlarged into a full volume, *Biblical Authority for Today*, which was edited by Wolfgang Schweitzer and Alan Richardson. The work shows clearly that no one answer for all denominations has yet been given concerning the nature of Biblical authority. Absence of unanimity on these matters indicates all the more clearly the importance of a fresh look at the church's origins, particularly with a view to her authority.

Mediation of Authority

There is, of course, a way of answering the question "By what authority?" that avoids the heart of the problem and fails to fathom the dilemma of the early Christians. One can hastily respond, "God is the ultimate authority!" True, Christianity's affirmation of belief in the triune God who reveals Himself to men grounds the problem of truth in the nature of God and in his self-revelation. All Christians agree on this. But *how* does God mediate his authority? This was the exhausting controversy of second-century Christians. In fact they could take us one step further than that without creating any noticeable reaction among their contemporaries. Christians universally asserted that the revelation of God the Father, brought to men by Jesus Christ, was delivered by the Holy Spirit to chosen men called "apostles."

The apostles seemed to early believers like a "multiplication of the Christ" to borrow a phrase from Adolf Harnack. One interesting illustration of this respect for the apostles has been preserved for us in the writings of the early historian Eusebius.[3] He tells us that when Bishop Serapion of Antioch (d.211) first heard of the so-called *Gospel of Peter* he accepted it temporarily as authoritative because claims were put forward so strongly that it was apostolic. But in order to make sure he went to Rhossos, where the book was circulating. Upon investigation he found it to be of a late date and of Gnostic origin. Thereupon he declared it to be false and

[3] Eusebius, *Ecclesiastical History* (from this point designated E.H.), VI, 12.

to possess no apostolic (divine) authority. The reaction was typical.

The same veneration of the Twelve and Paul is revealed by Ignatius, an earlier bishop of Antioch. Writing to the Romans he says, "I do not order you as did Peter and Paul; they were apostles, I am a convict, they were free, I am even until now a slave" (Rom. 4:3). But perhaps the most pointed paragraph of all in this connection is from the pen of the North African lawyer, Tertullian. He writes:

> We . . . are not permitted to cherish any object after our own will, nor yet to make choice of that which another has introduced of his private fancy. In the Lord's Apostles we possess our authority; for even they did not of themselves choose to introduce anything, but faithfully delivered to the nations [of mankind] the doctrine which they had received from Christ (*Prescription* 6).

Here Tertullian explains why the apostles are authoritative. They were first-hand witnesses of Christ. Their words, therefore, are to be accepted as the words of the Lord Himself. Another noteworthy fact is Tertullian's assumption that all innovation in matters of doctrine is outlawed. The voluble lawyer and his catholic contemporaries believed that orthodoxy was temporally prior to heresy. Unbelief, they felt, could only arise as an offshoot of apostolic truth. H.E.W. Turner calls this the "classical theory of the origin of heresy." Whatever allowance we make today for historical development, this "classical theory" has the merit of reminding us of the unchanging factor in theology. We cannot claim the support of the early church if we do not believe that "in the Lord's apostles we possess our authority." In the minds of early Christians, as Harnack has written, "There could be no doubt that the needful thing was to fix what was 'Apostolic,' for the one certain thing was that Christianity was based on a divine revelation which had been transmitted through the medium of the Apostles to the churches of the whole earth."[4]

Apostolic Standards

Yet in saying, "in the Lord's apostles we possess our authority," we have scarcely introduced our problem, because

[4] A. Harnack, *History of Dogma*, II, 25.

the church found more than one apostolic standard. Christians looked to an apostolic rule of faith, an apostolic succession of teachers, an apostolic canon of Scripture, and later an "apostles' creed." Determining the precise relationships among these various norms is no easy task. Harnack claimed that one of the most important problems to be investigated in the history of dogma is to show what relation was established between the apostolic rule of faith, the apostolic canon of Scripture, and the apostolic office. Our attempt to trace the interplay between these standards of authority demands that we first define four important terms: creed, rule of faith, tradition, and canon of Scripture.

The Creed

That creeds have a vital part to play in any consideration of authority is unquestioned. Even those who assert that they have no creed often upon examination manifest a rigid adherence to fairly definable dogmas. The issue turns less on acceptance or rejection of creeds and more on the role that creeds play in a pattern of authority. Here, of course, the lines are drawn today. Orthodoxy and the Roman Church claim absolute authority for their particular creedal statements. They only differ over what is included under that authority. The Eastern Church confines the claim of infallibility to the seven ecumenical Councils, from the first Council of Nicea in 325, to the second of Nicea in 787. The convert to Roman Catholicism, on the other hand, is required to

> accept and profess without doubting, the traditions, definitions and declarations of the sacred Canons and Oecumenical Councils and especially those of the holy Council of Trent (and the oecumenical Vatican Council, especially the definitions concerning the primacy of the Roman Pontiff and his infallible authority [magisterio]).[5]

Thus the difference in the two bodies turns upon the doctrine of papal infallibility. The Roman Church not only accepts

[5] The Tridentine Profession of Faith, 1564, from the Bull of Pius IV *Injunctum nobis*. For text see *Canon and Decrees of the Council of Trent*, H. J. Schroeder, O. P., p. 540. The parenthesis was added by order of Pope Pius IX in a decree of January 20, 1877 (*Acta Sanctae Sedis*, X, 71).

the confessions of the first seven ecumenical Councils and the subsequent ones defined by her, but accepts any future decisions of the Pope on matters of faith and morals as well.

In Protestant churches the authority of creeds is relative and limited, being subordinate to the Bible. Their value depends to a great extent upon the measure of their agreement with the Holy Scriptures.

Any creed in the sense in which we have been speaking here is universally authoritative within the church accepting it. This type of creed came into being at the Council of Nicea in 325 because only after the union of church and state under Constantine could any real universality be achieved. Prior to the fourth century all creeds and confessions were local in character and rested upon the local church for their authority, though, of course, it was assumed that they stated the universally accepted faith of the church. With Nicea, creeds in our modern sense of the word were introduced. In the words of C. H. Turner, "the old creeds were creeds for catechumens, the new creed was a creed for bishops."[6] This distinction is imperative if we are to understand the second-century scheme of authority. What Turner calls the "creed for bishops" simply does not exist in the early years of Christianity. His "creed for catechumens," however, deserves a further word.

Oscar Cullmann distinguishes between two types of early confession on the basis of the constituent wording of the statement.[7] One type is drawn up in the language of the New Testament, and is ascribed to the apostles as an authentic summary of the Scriptures. The Apostles' Creed is an example of this type. The other type takes up a position over against the heresies and problems of the time, as the Nicaeno-Constantinopolitan Creed. In this second type the biblical gospel is translated into the language and concepts of a certain period. Cullmann's distinction is quite helpful. There is some evidence that this "translation" of the gospel into the concepts of the time began in the second century.

For our purposes, however, another distinction, one em-

---

[6] C. H. Turner, *History and Use of Creeds and Anathemas*, p. 24. Quoted by J. N. D. Kelly, *Early Christian Creeds*, p. 205.
[7] O. Cullmann, *Early Christian Confessions*, p. 10.

INTRODUCTION 19

ployed by J.N.D. Kelly, is even more helpful.[8] In the earliest Christian decades, a time when conciliar creeds were unknown, we may distinguish declaratory creeds from interrogatory ones. The former were short statements couched in the first person professing belief in a select group of doctrines or facts considered to be of vital importance. This type was common in the preparation of catechumens for baptism. The interrogatory creeds were declarations of assent in answer to questions addressed to the candidates during the baptismal rite itself. Evidence indicates that declaratory creeds grew out of the interrogatory ones sometime in the third century. Because of their practical role in committing a believer to a standard of Christian orthodoxy, both types played a significant role in the pattern of authority.

The Rule of Faith

A second troublesome term found in pivotal passages in the early Fathers is the phrase "rule of faith" or "rule of truth." The exact meaning of the expression has been much debated by scholars of this subject. It was assumed by writers in the early part of our century that the rule of faith was identical with the creed and was a developed expression of the early baptismal formula. This assumption did not go unchallenged, but the position was widely influential. In more recent years, however, serious questions raised against this assumption have reopened the problem of the true nature of the rule. We now know that the creed was not fixed by the end of the second century, and the baptismal questions must have varied from place to place. The rule of faith, however, at least according to Tertullian, was everywhere and always the same (*Veiling of Virgins* 1). Furthermore, the rule included articles of faith not found in the known baptismal confessions. Any study of the statements of the rule will show as much. For these reasons any attempt to identify directly the rule with the baptismal confession is doomed to failure.

Irenaeus attributes the rule to the apostles (*Against Heresies* I,10,1 and II,4,1) and Tertullian traces it back to the

[8] Kelly, *op. cit.*, ch. II.

Lord himself (*Presc.* 13). At first glance such claims resemble the fourth-century practice of attributing the articles of the creed to the apostles. Later attestations to an "apostles' creed" must be dismissed as naive legend. But we may take Irenaeus and Tertullian quite seriously if we do not identify the rule with the creed. It is best to consider the rule as a brief, flexible summation of the fundamentals of the church's faith. Since it is a series of ideas rather than a precisely worded creed it may well claim to be apostolic. In this sense it is practically synonymous with the doctrinal summation of "the tradition."

Tradition

Tradition, as usage shows, is an extremely flexible term. One widely used sense of the word today connotes "the customary way of doing it." In this sense we speak of fireworks on July 4 or turkey on Thanksgiving as "traditional." The basic idea here seems to be long and continuous practice. Tradition in this sense is practically equal to custom. Custom as a source of truth, however, received no sanction in the early church. In the words of Cyprian, venerated Bishop of Carthage, "custom without truth is the antiquity of error." The early Christians understood something else than this when they used "tradition."

In Catholic theological vocabulary the word means "the ongoing life of the church" or, as in Roman Catholicism, the organ by which Christian truth is transmitted, the *magisterium* or living authority of the Church. As we noted above, whatever shade of meaning the word may carry it must be given serious consideration as a source of authority.

Tradition (*paradosis*, literally a "handing over") is frequently used in the New Testament. For example, Judas "hands over" Jesus to the Jewish leaders and they in turn "hand him over" to Pilate. When applied to teaching it refers to the Lord's Supper or to the gospel that Paul "handed over" to the Corinthians (I Cor. 11:2, 23; 15:3) and to the faith that Jude declares is once "handed over" to the saints (Jude 3).

Perhaps the most illuminating biblical passage is Mark 7:1-13 where Jesus condemns the Jewish leaders for leaving

Introduction

the commands of God for the "traditions" of men (Mark 7:8). Jesus cannot be censuring these religious rulers for passing on their teaching from one generation to the next, since Scripture itself, which Jesus accepted, was "handed over" in just this way. The scribes' blameworthiness rested rather in their failure to distinguish the word delivered by God from the doctrines imposed by men. Source determined authority! That is why the term, in spite of Jewish misuse, remained a suitable word for designating Christian teaching. Christian "tradition," unlike Jewish dogma, was from the Lord. Hence the essential idea behind "tradition" is not "transmission," the handing down of a doctrine from one person to the next, but initial "delivery." Thus applied to Christian doctrine, "tradition" is that teaching delivered by Jesus Christ and his apostles.

Tradition in this sense must at first have been entirely oral. Only after a number of years was it written down. By Luke's day so many reports are afield that he feels compelled to write in order to set the record straight for Theophilus (Luke 1:1-4). Thus for a time both forms of the tradition existed side by side as Paul's admonition to the Thessalonians shows (II Thess. 2:15). The Gospels and Epistles did not force oral tradition from the Christian consciousness entirely. The two remained coordinate sources of the one message. Even as late as the third decade of the second century Papias still had confidence in oral reports. He wrote, "If ever anyone came who had followed the presbyters, I inquired into the words of the presbyters . . . for I did not suppose that information from books would help me so much as the word of a living and surviving voice."[9]

During the earliest years of the church, then, the issue was not so much a question of either oral or written tradition as it was of both forms constituting the same tradition. There was no sense of discord between the two. They were two forms of the same thing. The basic question, and the one upon which fundamental authority depended, was — What is apostolic? — because apostolic tradition was the divine truth delivered by Jesus Christ.

---

[9] Eusebius, *E.H.*, III, 39.

Canon of Scripture

The same word translated "rule" (*kanōn*) in the phrase "rule of faith" is also applied to an exclusive selection of Christian writings for use in public worship. In the Greek language the word was often employed of a carpenter's tool, one used to determine the right direction of a piece of wood or a stone. It was also used of the scribe's ruler, translated by the Latin *regula*. From this literal sense of ruler or level the metaphorical senses derived. In the second-century church it came to designate, as we have seen, that body of Christian teachings to which one's life and doctrine must conform, the rule of truth or faith.

The regular use of the word in connection with the Bible first appears in the middle of the fourth century. Athanasius, the much-harassed Alexandrian Bishop, employs the word in this sense in his *Decrees of the Synod of Nicea* and in his famous *Easter Letter* of 367. But the idea of a canon of Scripture is much earlier than the use of the word.

The concept of a canon in the sense of a list of books that may be read in public religious services is derived by the church from Judaism. The canonical Old Testament consisted of three parts: Law, Prophets, and Writings. The history of the Old Testament canon is a tedious problem into which we cannot enter here. Whenever the process may have been "completed," the idea antedated the coming of Jesus, and the church quite naturally received the Palestinian list of books that Jesus accepted.

The formal recognition of a fixed list, or canon, of New Testament writings can be dated about the middle of the second century. Apparently, the first to draft such a list was the heretic Marcion, who left the Catholic Church in Rome in 144. In the controversy that followed his departure the word frequently used to designate documents of divine revelation was *diathēkē*, a "covenant" or "compact" between God and man. The "Old Testament" became the collection of documents testifying to the earlier "covenant" between God and Abraham and God and Moses, while the "New Testament" came to refer to the books testifying to the "covenant" sealed by Jesus' blood. By Irenaeus' time writers speak unequivocally of a "New" Testament parallel to the

INTRODUCTION 23

"Old" (*A.H.* IV,9,1). Thus, while the precise limits of the New Testament canon were still very much a matter of debate, the idea of such a canon was firmly established by the end of the second century. As was true of tradition and the rule of faith, the supreme test of canonicity was apostolicity. The relation of these various apostolic standards to one another is the subject of the study in the following pages.

Setting the limits for a study of this type is always a bit of a problem. We have chosen to develop the theme to the early decades of the third century. There are certain reasons for this terminal point. First, the full canonical status of most of the Christian writings was recognized by the closing decades of the second century, and the description of them as the "New Testament" had come into vogue.

Second, shortly after the beginning of the third century the episcopate, especially in the West, becomes the guardian of the Christian revelation. By the middle of the third century Cyprian can write: "You should know that the bishop is in the church and the church in the bishop, and that if anyone is not with the bishop he is not in the church" (*Epistle* LXVI,7). This view of the institutional church adds a whole new network of considerations that would compound our study.

Third, the writers included here carry us through the reaction of the church to Marcionism and the problem of the canon and through Gnosticism and the problem of exegesis. Subsequent debates on the problem of authority have swirled about the basic issues raised in these controversies: secret and apostolic tradition, episcopal and apostolic succession, creeds and the rule of faith, the canon and the living voice of the church.

Fourth, by entering the third century sufficiently to hear the testimony of the Alexandrians, we gain a wider witness geographically. We then have voices from Gaul, Rome, North Africa, and Egypt, and where unanimity emerges from them we can be confident that the testimony represents the mind of the church.

The particular arrangement of the material is also not without purpose. The same information could have been treated topically throughout but, because the average reader is less familiar with the Fathers than might be desired, we have chosen this arrangement in order to introduce each writer before hearing his testimony. We move, therefore, from the apostolic age through the writings of the Apostolic Fathers, the Apologists, Irenaeus, Tertullian, and the Alexandrians.

II

THE EARLY SECOND CENTURY: THE APOSTOLIC FATHERS (Part I)

"APOSTOLIC FATHERS" IS NOT AN ALTOGETHER HAPPY NAME for that group of Christians who wrote during the early decades of the second century. Though several of these men did have first-hand contact with the apostles, they were not "apostolic" in the accepted sense of the word. They were neither the recipients of revelation, as the Twelve and Paul, nor were they commissioned for special missionary service. All the same, the label has found its place in Patristic study, and after many years it is not likely to give way to a more appropriate title.

The writings are marked by variety both in style and in content. There are several letters, a sermon, a church manual, a martyrdom narrative, and an apocalypse. In fact, other than their nearness to the apostolic age there is little reason to consider them collectively. But because of this proximity to the fount of Christianity they are an indispensable source of information on the problem of authority at that time. They reflect the vitality of a generation deeply impressed by a majestic memory but are content to echo what they had seen and heard.

The citations of Scripture in the Apostolic Fathers are especially noteworthy. Usually when any of the authors quotes a New Testament writer he does so without exhibiting the apostle's authority. His true attitude toward apostolic testimony is revealed less in his direct quotations than in his allusions and in his habit of interweaving biblical terminology with his own. Part of the explanation of this use of Holy Writ lies in the purpose of the writers. "Scriptural language," as G. D. Barry has put it, "is introduced for purposes of exhortation and not of controversy."[1] While the sub-apostolic church was not unaware of heresy, the Marcionite and Gnostic disputants, who later called forth an unambiguous announcement of catholic doctrinal standards, had not yet lifted their voices.

In our study, therefore, we must seek what the Apostolic Fathers imply as well as what they assert. "The first literature of a church," B. F. Westcott reminds us, "is practical rather than doctrinal, and we must endeavor to discover the teaching, which it involves, rather than merely that which it expresses."[2] Pursue this course in the Apostolic Fathers and the results are convincing. A careful study reveals their high regard for the New Testament witness. "Within the compass of a few brief letters," writes Bishop Westcott, "they show that the writings of the Apostles were regarded from the first as invested with singular authority, as the true expression, if not the original source, of Christian doctrine and Christian practice."[3] But if we are to support this generalization we must turn to the individual writers themselves.

I. DIDACHE

The *Didache,* as we now have it, is a church manual that purports to give the teachings of the Lord as handed down through the twelve apostles. F. L. Cross calls it "the most interesting discovery in the field of Patristic literature in the last hundred years." The first part of the *Didache,* called "The Two Ways" (chs. 1-6), is a bit of catechetical instruction

---

[1] G. D. Barry, *Inspiration and Authority,* p. 35.
[2] B. F. Westcott, *Introduction to the Study of the Gospel,* p. 403.
[3] B. F. Westcott, *History of the Canon of the New Testament,* p. 21.

to be read by those who are seeking church membership and who "wish to be instructed in the way of godliness." The second part (chs. 7-15) gives a series of instructions concerning Christian worship, and the standards for the discrimination of apostles and prophets. Finally, in view of eschatological events, a warning is appended.[4] Taken as a unit the book witnesses to the early use of apostolic teaching in Christian liturgy and in the Scriptures and to a Spirit-endowed ministry.

Christ and Apostolic Teaching

The fact that the book purports to contain the teaching of Jesus Christ delivered through the apostles is in itself significant. It shows that in the mind of early believers it was pre-eminently through the apostles that the Lord delivered his truth to the church. At the same time the use of "apostle" to designate those who with early Christian prophets traveled around from place to place preaching and teaching (11:3-6) indicates that the term was not restricted to the Twelve.

While apostolic doctrine is nowhere explicitly defined, some norm for Christian truth is assumed. The reader is admonished (by a reference to a warning in Deuteronomy 4:2) not to forsake the commandments of the Lord (4:3), is warned against teaching "without God" (6:1), and is urged to accept *as the Lord* itinerant preachers who teach things contained in the manual, and to shun those who teach contrary to it (11:1-8). The big question about the sources from which this doctrine is drawn is not disclosed. It was simply "the teaching of the Lord."

This means that any search in the *Didache* for explicit statements concerning tradition is unrewarding. Neither the noun nor the verb is used in the sense of teaching. In only one place is there any hint of the instruction or confession associated with the baptismal rite. Giving directions for the

---

[4] The apparent composite character of the document complicates an already complex problem of its date. The original "Teaching" is very probably from the first century, while the second recension is roughly contemporary with Polycarp. The similarities of the "Two Ways" section to the *Epistle of Barnabas* suggests their mutual dependence upon a pre-Christian Jewish document. See recent views in F. L. Cross, *Early Christian Fathers*, pp. 8-11.

administration of baptism the author says, "Having first rehearsed all these things, baptize in running water in the name of the Father and of the Son and of the Holy Spirit" (7:1).[5] Evidently a threefold interrogatory confession was in vogue here, because baptism was administered by three successive applications of water (7:3).

Scripture

Direct quotations of Scripture are likewise infrequent. Only two appear in the whole book. Once the author quotes Malachi 1:11, 14, introducing it by the clause "This is that which was spoken by the Lord" (14:3). And another time he quotes Zechariah 14:5 following the formula "as it was said" (16:7). This scanty use of the Old Testament may be attributed to the purpose of the writer to set forth the teaching of the Lord to the Gentiles. And, though they are few, these references are enough to indicate the author's high regard for the old covenant.

In addition to these direct quotes there are four references to the "gospel" with written documents in view (8:2; 11:3; 15:3-4). One of these alludes to Jesus' instruction on prayer in Matthew 6:9-13. In another, Matthew 7:6 is quoted after the words "This also did the Lord say." In every case, however, the singular form "gospel" is used, suggesting that the unity of the source rather than the individual writings was in view. Moreover, the words of Christ are not always properly understood. T. F. Torrance has pointed out that, "while the *Didache* claims to go back to the words of our Lord, these are torn out of their context and fitted into another scheme in which they lose their original force and meaning."[6] Still it cannot be doubted that in practice "the words of the Lord" carried as much authority for the author of the *Didache* as did the Old Testament.

Nor do direct quotations tell the whole story of the im-

[5] The meaning of "these things" will depend upon the view taken of the composition of the *Didache*. If there is no break at this point "these things" may mean chapters 1-6; if there is a break, we are left to speculation.

[6] T. F. Torrance, *The Doctrine of Grace in the Apostolic Fathers*, p. 38.

portance of "the words of the Lord" for this unknown author. Frequently we find verbal agreement between the *Didache* and our New Testament. While such phrases used do not manifest any conscious effort to quote authoritatively, they do reveal a familiarity with the record of the Lord's life and teaching. Use of the accounts had become an unconscious "second-nature." This is true not only of the *Didache* but of the other Apostolic Fathers as well. In the absence of controversy and the need to formulate any explicit doctrine of Scripture, this freedom in echoing the New Testament is a valuable witness to the position the apostolic writings so rapidly achieved in the church.

The Spirit and the Ministry

Finally, the major problem related to authority and raised by the *Didache* is the work of the Spirit in the church. What authority rested upon charismatic men in this early age? Aside from the bishops and deacons appointed by the church (15:1) three offices are mentioned: apostles, prophets, and teachers (10:7; 11:3-11; 13:1-6; 15:1-2). Apparently some Christians held these men in high esteem, since the *Didache* exhorts the church (as though there were some reluctance) to receive bishops and deacons as they do prophets and teachers (15:1-2). Our problem is, what relation did these Spirit-filled men have to the "teaching of the Lord"?

The book gives certain tests by which false prophets may be identified (11:8). At the same time, however, the church is admonished not to test or examine any prophet who is speaking in the Spirit. To do so is to commit the unpardonable sin (11:7). How can these two directives be reconciled? Flesseman-Van Leer suggests that the criteria given are not really human standards and may therefore be used in distinguishing the false prophet from the true.[7] The Spirit is in no way tested, only he who falsely claims to have the Spirit. When the church is told to ignore anyone who teaches any other doctrine (11:1-2) than that taught in the *Didache*, it is not the Spirit that is judged by true doctrine, but he who

[7] E. Flesseman-Van Leer, *Tradition and Scripture in the Early Church*, p. 17.

is filled with the Spirit will show that he is so filled by his proper teaching and conduct. The Spirit and the teaching of the Lord are therefore coordinate authorities, one unable to exist without the other.[8]

For our purpose the basic issue is this: Was there a teaching given by these "apostles and prophets" that was equal in authority to the teaching of the Lord through the Twelve and Paul? One thing is clear from the New Testament. The possession of the Spirit for a particular function by anyone in the early church did not assure him authority in matters of doctrine. According to Paul every member of the church who manifests any "grace" does so as a "charisma." The real issue in the *Didache*, then, is whether or not these itinerant teachers taught authoritative doctrine other than that of the Lord through the apostles. If this is so, the answer must be in the negative. In the words of J. A. Robinson, "We dispute . . . the theory that at any period there existed a 'triad' of apostles, prophets, and teachers with a personal preeminence and a recognized claim to honour. Such a preeminence remains undisputed for the Apostles."[9]

II. I CLEMENT

The epistle commonly known as *I Clement* was written in the name of the Roman Church by the bishop of the Roman Christians, Clement. It seems that the old problem of party spirit at Corinth had persisted after the death of Paul, and the presbyters (elders) appointed by the apostles or their immediate successors had been deposed by the church. The letter from Rome, written near the close of the persecution under Domitian (A.D. 96), was sent as a rebuke for this hasty action.

Roman Catholic scholars find in this intervention "the Epiphany of the Roman Primacy."[10] James A. Kleist says

---

[8] The issue here in the *Didache* is parallel to that of I Cor. 14 where Paul does not deny the gifts of the Spirit but speaks as though they in no way surpass or set aside apostolic authority and teaching.

[9] J. A. Robinson, "The Church Ministry," in H. B. Swete (ed.) *Essays on the History of the Church and the Ministry*, p. 78.

[10] P. Batiffol, *L'Eglise naissante*, p. 146, quoted in J. Lebreton and J. Zeiller, *The History of the Primitive Church*, I, 413.

that "Clement speaks as though he were conscious of being more than the bishop of another diocese."[11] Protestant scholars, on the other hand, are less ready to find any particular jurisdictional authority beyond Rome. In any case there is no need to enter the controversy here. The position one takes bears upon the problem of authority, but since Clement does not claim to be a source of authoritative teaching, the problem is not a central issue for us. We are interested in Clement's view of Scripture, tradition, and the bishop.

Scripture

Clement is aware of a body of teachings that declare the Christian's responsibility to God (1:3; 3:4; 40:4; 58:2). He calls them commands and ordinances of the Lord "written on the tables of your heart" (2:8), or, as on one occasion, "the commands of Jesus" (49:1). Just as God teaches through Jesus (59:3), so also Christ speaks through his Spirit in the words of the Old Testament (22:1) and in the message of his apostles. The apostles were especially important as founders of churches.

> Having therefore received their commands, and being fully assured by the resurrection of our Lord Jesus Christ, and with their faith confirmed by the word of God, they went forth in the assurance of the Holy Spirit preaching the good news that the Kingdom of God is coming (42).

Clement knows, however, that this ministry was not limited to preaching, since he says that the apostles also wrote epistles (47:1-3).

Therefore, if he does not quote the apostles as he does the Old Testament it is not because of his ignorance of their writings. On the contrary, his letter reveals a thorough knowledge of them. Does he not encourage the Church at Corinth to take up the letter of the blessed Paul, the apostle (47:1)? By a study of Clement's style, vocabulary, and doctrine Westcott finds several apostolic traditions — Pauline, Petrine, Johannine — combined in his letter.[12] Thus, when he quotes the apostolic writings freely, he is not unconscious

---

[11] J. A. Kleist, *Ancient Christian Writers*, I, note on I Clement 59:1.
[12] Westcott, *History of Canon*, pp. 25-26.

of their authority. Usually he introduces an excerpt by "remember the words of the Lord Jesus" (13:1; 46:7). And to the early Christian there was no higher court of appeal.

We find a good example of how Clement used his sources of authority in chapter thirteen. He exhorts his readers to humbleness of mind because of "that which stands written" in Jeremiah 9:23-24. Then he adds "especially remembering the words of the Lord Jesus" and proceeds to quote several verses from Matthew and Luke (Matt. 5:7; 6:14; 7:2, 12; and Luke 6:31, 36-38). He then concludes, "With this commandment and with these injunctions let us strengthen ourselves to walk in obedience to his hallowed words." Evidently both the Old Testament reference and the words of Jesus are included in "commandment and injunction." Moreover, if we can place any weight upon the "especially" (*malista*), the words of Jesus are in no way inferior to the Old Testament authority. Both are to Clement the voice of the Lord.

We gain a further insight into the form of God's revelation from the three occasions when Clement uses the word *logia* ("oracle" in 19:1; 53:1; 62:3). Though Scripture may not be directly identified with this term, each of these instances surrounds it with connotations of Holy Writ. In chapter 19:1 Clement speaks of the generations before his time who received "his [God's] oracles" in fear and truth. In chapter 53:1 he says, "you have a good understanding of the Sacred Scriptures, beloved, and you have studied the oracles of God." And in chapter 62:3 he asserts that he is writing to men who "had studied the oracles of God." Taken together the three statements emphasize Clement's view that God has delivered a propositional revelation that is accessible to man in the Scriptures.

The particular method God used in delivering this revelation was through the inspiration of biblical writers. The Holy Spirit was the ultimate author of the Scriptures. They were given through him (45:2), and it is he who speaks in the words of the Scriptures (13:1; 16:2). Put in another way, "the ministers of the grace of God spoke through the Holy Spirit" (8:1). For this reason the Scriptures can be called "holy" and "true" (13:3; 56:3; 45:2). Since the Old Testament was thus inspired by the Christian's God, Clement finds the Christian message in it throughout, sometimes in the most obscure detail, such as in Rahab's scarlet thread (12:7). This belief in the work of the Spirit seems to create a problem at one point. In concluding his letter Clement tells the Corinthians that he has written them "through the Holy Spirit" (63:2). Did he believe that he too was inspired? It hardly seems consistent with the rest of his letter (7:1) and particularly with his high regard for the apostles (42) to understand his claim to be writing "through the Holy Spirit" as in any sense a claim of equality with the biblical writers. There is no need to see in this any more inspiration than that granted to any believer.[13] The Bishop's unguarded comment is what one might expect from an age that had not yet forged a technical theological vocabulary. His use of "tradition" reveals a similar nontechnical language.

Tradition

Though he employs the verb *paradidonai* (to hand over) twelve times, none of these is in the sense of deliverance of teaching. The one possible exception is in chapter 51:2, where he says that some are willing to suffer torture and blame of themselves rather than of "our tradition of noble and righteous harmony." But here Clement has in mind the Christians' practice of living peaceably with one another rather than any idea of doctrinal teaching.

The noun form occurs only once in his letter but then, interestingly, it is combined with *kanōn*. In chapter 7:2 he writes, "Let us come to the glorious and venerable rule of our tradition." Though Lightfoot translates this "rule which hath been handed down to us," there seems to be no thought in Clement of a creed or rule of faith.[14] The context, which issues a call to repentance, is loaded with ethical and moral overtones. "Let us review all the generations," he urges, "and let us learn that in generation after generation the Master has given a place of repentance to those who will turn to him." It is best therefore to consider this "rule of

---

[13] Flesseman-Van Leer, *op. cit.*, pp. 24-25. J. B. Lightfoot, holding that the letter is from the whole Church, makes this a claim of the whole Church. *Apostolic Fathers*, 5 vols., I, 2, 170, n. 5.

[14] Lightfoot, *Apostolic Fathers*, 1 vol., p. 60.

tradition" as more ethical than doctrinal. Certainly it is no rule of faith.

This is not to suggest that Clement was ignorant of apostolic tradition. The main events of Christ's life and death are known to him: Christ's descent according to the flesh (32:2), his humility (16:2), his suffering (2:1), his death for our salvation (7:4; 12:7), and his resurrection (24:1; 42:3). These events could be designated tradition, but Clement does not call them this and he never suggests how they are known.

We do find in Clement, as we do in other Apostolic Fathers, brief creed-like phrases. One example is in chapter 46 where Clement, prompted by the divisive contentiousness of the Corinthians, writes: "Have we not one God, and one Christ, and one Spirit of grace which has been poured upon us?" Furthermore, he reminds them, we have "one calling in Christ." This probably reflects the baptismal setting where the Spirit was poured upon believers, but without firm evidence we cannot be sure that Clement knew of any confession independent of the Scriptures.

The Bishop

The last matter to consider in this letter from Rome is the role of the bishop. Did, according to Clement, apostolic authority in any sense reside in the bishop? Does *I Clement* support the primacy of Rome? Is there evidence of an apostolic succession continued by the work of the Holy Spirit?

Though Clement is aware of the bishop's office (44:1) he never uses the term *episkopos* (bishop) in the singular to designate an individual. There is, therefore, no evidence of a monarchical episcopacy in Clement. That much is quite clear. It is equally noteworthy that the terms *episkopos* and *presbuteros* (elder) are in his book synonymous, as they are in the New Testament (44:5).

The two passages especially important for a study of the bishop's office are chapters forty-two and forty-four. In chapter forty-two Clement declares that the apostles preached from district to district and "appointed their firstfruits, when they had proved them by the Spirit, to be bishops and deacons unto future believers." As the participle "proved" (*dokimasantes*) indicates, the Spirit's activity mentioned here was upon the apostles, not upon the bishops. Elsewhere in Clement's letter he does suggest that grace has been given to the leaders of the church, but only because they are humble (30:2-3). Therefore, we cannot consider this a unique ministerial gift because grace, according to Clement, is poured upon all believers (46:6). Grace was simply "the effluent influence of the Spirit within a united church."[15]

We must also note before leaving chapter forty-two that there is here no suggestion that the teaching and preaching of the apostles continued through the bishops. There is no reason to doubt that the early bishops were heralds of the apostolic message, but that was not Clement's primary interest. He saw them as leaders of Christian worship.

Chapter forty-four supports this view. Here Clement asserts that the apostles "provided a continuance, that if these [the apostles' successors] should fall asleep other approved men should succeed to their ministry." That a succession is in view here cannot be questioned, but there is not a hint that it is an apostolic-episcopal succession transmitting a gift for interpreting Christian truth. The gift mentioned includes cultic functions, but there is no suggestion of a doctrinal or ethical authority beyond that demanded by the bishop's own blameless character (44:3). C. H. Turner's conclusion is the only valid one: "The only succession of which Clement speaks is in so many words the succession of presbyters to their predecessor in office in the local church."[16]

III. IGNATIUS

According to the early church historian Eusebius, Ignatius was the third bishop of Antioch in Syria. He was condemned as a Christian and sent to Rome to face the beasts in the amphitheater (*E.H.* III,22). His journey to the imperial capital took him through various towns in Asia Minor where he penned letters to the churches of other cities. While at Smyrna he wrote to the believers at Ephesus, Magnesia, Tralles, and Rome, and later when he reached Troas he wrote to Philadelphia, Smyrna, and to the Bishop of the

---

[15] Torrance, *op. cit.*, p. 53.
[16] C. H. Turner, "Apostolic Succession," in Swete, *op. cit.*, p. 112.

Church at Smyrna, Polycarp. Taken collectively the epistles reveal the early development of confessions, the use of the gospel, and the role of the bishop as defenses against heresy. Though the exact date of Ignatius' martyrdom is debated, it was sometime during the reign of Trajan (A.D. 98-117).

Christ and the Apostles

For Ignatius, Jesus Christ is the bringer of knowledge (*gnosis*), a teacher and law-giver, yet he is more. He is himself *gnosis*, God's unerring mouthpiece (*Rom.* 8:2). And since the apostles followed him completely, he spoke through them (*Mag.* 7:1) and used their precepts as his own (*Mag.* 13:1). Thus apostolic authority rests upon absolute obedience to Jesus Christ (*Mag.* 13:2).

Creeds

The main tenets of this apostolic message appear in Ignatius' letters in brief creedlike statements. These are obviously phrased so as to guard the believers from impending heresy. For example, the word "truly" occurs four times in one brief statement concerning Christ (*Tral.* 9) and is almost certainly directed against the teaching that the eternal Son only appeared to be human (docetism). Similar statements occur elsewhere in the Bishop's epistles (*Smyrn.* 1, *Mag.* 11; *Eph.* 18). Usually these are christological confessions, but Ignatius is acquainted with trinitarian ones as well (*Mag.* 13).

Assembling these confessions some scholars have attempted to reconstruct "the creed of St. Ignatius." While this is a futile undertaking, it is possible to trace the outlines of a christological *kerygma* or the early catechetical instruction. As C. H. Turner writes, we are not to think that Ignatius had any apostolic creed or code of apostolic canons in mind, but he did believe that apostolic authority lay behind the Christian system of his day.[17] He was setting forth the essence (though not theoretically elaborated) of the rule of faith, and employing it as later writers will as a norm for Christianity in the face of threatening heresy.

[17] *Ibid.*, p. 114.

Scripture

In his conflict with unbelief Ignatius also has recourse to the Scriptures. Though not often quoting them directly, he nevertheless reveals his submission to their authority. In speaking of heretics who deny the meaning of the eucharist, he says that it is right to refrain from such men and "to give heed to the prophets and especially to the gospel, in which the Passion has been revealed to us and the Resurrection has been accomplished" (*Smyrn.* 7:2). Thus according to the Bishop there are two major sources of doctrine: the prophets and the gospel.

The "divine prophets" lived according to Jesus Christ and were inspired by his grace, their purpose and mission being "to convince the disobedient that there is one God, who manifested himself through Jesus Christ his son" (*Mag.* 8:2). In fact, these prophets announced the gospel, hoped in Christ, waited for him, and were united with him (*Phila.* 5:2). Since God so used the prophets, Christians should give them heed (*Smyrn.* 7:2).

Ignatius' basic authority, however, is "the gospel." Though direct quotations of the New Testament are not found in his letters, this fact alone, as we noted in Clement, will not give us a true picture of apostolic authority. We find at least one saying directly attributed to the Lord (*Smyrn.* 3:2). In all probability it is a traditional saying based upon Luke 24:39. But of far greater import is the definite evidence of apostolic influence upon the Bishop's thought. Such evidence can not always be deduced from explicit statements. As with Clement, it is detected in similarities of vocabulary and style.[18] For example, the stamp of Paul can be observed in the language and doctrine of Ignatius and in his allusions to the great apostle's letters. And, as if to give us complete assurance of his knowledge of Paul, Ignatius explicitly refers to the writings of the apostle (*Eph.* 12:2). Similarly, Johannine tradition may be noted in such expressions as "the Word," the manifestation of God (*Mag.* 8:2), "the door of the Father" (*Phila.* 9:1), the Spirit "knoweth whence it comes and whither it goes" (*Phila.* 7:1), "the bread of God" (*Rom.*

---

[18] See the evidence gathered by Westcott, *op. cit.*, p. 33.

7:3), and "the ruler of this world" (*Rom.* 7:1). These certainly evince a knowledge of the Johannine mode of thought, if not of his actual writings.

Thus the two sources — the Old Testament and the "New" — form the foundation of Ignatius' thought and teaching. Basic to both is the all-important message of the gospel. Ignatius speaks of himself as "having fled to the gospel as to the flesh of Jesus, and to the apostles as to the presbytery of the church. Yes, and let us love the prophets also, because they also preached unto the gospel" (*Phila.* 5:1-2). The Bishop's shift here from gospel and apostles to the prophets is abrupt indeed if these, like the prophets, are not writings. At the same time we must note that he does use the singular form of "gospel." The message of the Evangelists in its unity was still foremost. Ignatius had not expressly distinguished his sources, though there seems to be no reason for denying him access to much of what we know today as the New Testament. The question is still not so much "either oral or written" as "both oral and written tradition." In Ignatius there is no hint of a conflict between the two.

Before leaving the subject of the Scriptures, we must deal with a passage that has caused much controversy. In the letter to the Philadelphians (8:2) the Antiochene leader reports that he had heard some say, "If I find it not in the charters, I do not believe in the gospel."[19] Whether from Christians with Judaistic tendencies or from a definite heretical sect, the appeal to "the charters" is apparently referring to the Old Testament, and is worded in such a way as to suggest a contrast to the gospel. Ignatius counters this appeal by asserting that it is written in the Old Testament (*gegraptai*). This appears to be the meaning of the verse for two reasons: (1) In no other instance do we find *gegraptai* referring to the gospel or to the New Testament. (2) Ignatius, as we have seen, believed that the gospel was in the Old Testament. Hence, he granted his opponents' demand, asserting that the gospel was in the Old Testament. They would not be convinced, however, and simply repeated the

---

[19] *En tōi euangeliōi* cannot be in apposition to *en tois archeiois*. Lightfoot, *Apostolic Fathers*, 5 vols., Part II, II, 2, 272.

question, "Is it?" To this Ignatius writes, "The charters are Jesus Christ, his death and resurrection."[20] He seems to say by this that for the Christian the gospel guarantees the use of the Old Testament, not vice versa. At least this interpretation of the passage has the merit of harmonizing with what the Bishop says elsewhere in his writings (*Smyrn.* 7:2; *Mag.* 13:1).

The Bishop

Throughout his works the problem of how to guard the gospel from impure hands was a disturbing one for Ignatius. He believed that his approaching death was at a critical time in the history of the church. His days were "the last days" (*Eph.* 11:1). With the death of the apostles a new crisis had fallen upon the church. This view helps to account for Ignatius' vehement support of episcopacy. Here, according to the great leader, was the bond of unity and safety for God's people. In the bishop the congregation is summed up (*Eph.* 1:3) and the basis of unity is found (*Mag.* 6:2). In fact, there is no valid meeting of the church without the bishop (*Mag.* 4:1). This unity centering in the bishop bears in turn upon doctrine.

While the Ignatian bishop is primarily a leader of Christian worship and the center of cultic unity, at least one reference (*Phila.* 3) ties liturgy to doctrine. He says, "For as many as are with God and Jesus Christ, these are with the bishop.... If any one follows a schismatic, he does not inherit the kingdom of God; if any man walks in strange doctrine, he has no part in the Passion."

Yet the fact that Ignatius is primarily concerned with the bishop's role as leader of the congregation's worship helps explain why there is no apostolic succession in his writings. C. H. Turner, noting this lack of a succession, points out the contrast with Clement.[21] As we saw, in Clement the succession was the succession of presbyters to their predecessors in the local church. Ignatius, on the other hand, pays no attention to this, but "has a very vivid sense of the individual

---

[20] For a similar understanding see Flesseman-Van Leer, *op. cit.*, p. 34. See also Robert M. Grant, *The Bible in the Church*, p. 44.
[21] In Swete, *op. cit.*, pp. 112-113.

bishop as the center of unity and in the background a sense of the sum total of these individual bishops as the expression of the mind of Jesus Christ in the Christian society." Some indeed have tried to find an early theory of succession in Ignatius.[22] They point to such passages as *Magnesians* 6:1, where the bishop is said to preside in the place of God and the presbyters in the place of the apostles. But a comparison of all such statements in Ignatius will show that the metaphor is often shifted. Once the bishop is in the place of the Father (*Tral.* 3:1), another time in the place of Christ. Such evidence is too shaky to support any real theory of historical succession. With Torrance we must conclude that grace resides with the bishop but not because it has been passed on to him by a predecessor. Rather, as head of the community he gathers up in himself the unity of the church.[23]

[22] E. Hatch, *Organization of the Earliest Christian Churches*, p. 89.
[23] Torrance, *op. cit.*, p. 88.

III

THE EARLY SECOND CENTURY: THE APOSTOLIC FATHERS (Part II)

IV. POLYCARP

POLYCARP, THE BISHOP OF SMYRNA IN THE FIRST HALF OF the second century, was martyred on February 23, A.D. 155 (or 156). When he met his fiery end he was at least eighty-six years old. Thus his life and ministry span the years between the apostolic age and the middle of the second century. Moreover, Irenaeus, who had sat at Polycarp's feet, tells us that the old Bishop had as a youth been personally acquainted with John, "the disciple of the Lord" (*A.H.* III, 3,4). Consequently, we have in the aged martyr a notable witness of the days immediately following the apostles.

The lone epistle from his hand that has survived the centuries was written (probably about 135) in reply to a communication from the Christians at Philippi (3:1). The Philippians had requested of Polycarp any exhortation he might have and any letters Ignatius might have sent to him (13:2). In his response the Pastor of Smyrna reveals his extensive use of the apostolic writings and of the growing importance of doctrinal summations of the faith.

He shows that the ultimate authority for him, both doctrinal and moral, is God or Jesus Christ. As Ignatius before him, Polycarp declares that Christians should obey the word of righteousness (9:1) and should walk in the commandment of the Lord according to his truth (4:1; 2:2; 5:1). Since the prophets proclaimed Christ's coming, and, since the apostles preached his gospel, both participate in the Lord's authority (6:3). Other than this Polycarp never mentions the prophets, though he does refer to the apostles again (3:2) when he confesses his inability to attain unto the wisdom "of the blessed and glorious Paul." Any hint of a succession to the apostles is lacking however.

Scripture

In his use of the Scriptures Polycarp resembles Clement of Rome. He has a habit of weaving scriptural phrases into his own writing without any conscious effort to quote. In only two instances does he explicitly refer to the words of the Lord. In chapter 2:3 he says, "remembering what the Lord taught when he said." Then a free quotation of several phrases from Matthew 7, 6, and 5 and from Luke 6 follows. The first clauses resemble *I Clement* 13, but differences suggest that the citations are not derived from any other source than our Gospels. In chapter 7:2 there is a final reference to the Lord's words. Though again quoted freely, they are definitely from our present Gospels (Matt. 6:13; 26:41).

Twice after an introductory phrase this respected Christian leader quotes from the Pauline letters. In citing I Corinthians 6:2 he adds, "as Paul teaches" (11:2); and later he introduces Psalm 4:5 and Ephesians 4:26 with "it is said in these Scriptures" (12:1). Whether or not Polycarp really considered this Pauline letter as "Scripture" may be debated.[1] But the evidence for his submission to the apostolic writings does not rest upon direct quotations alone.

His short epistle contains more indirect references to the writings of the New Testament than any other work of this age. And yet, with the exceptions of the above-mentioned

[1] Flesseman-Van Leer (*Tradition and Scripture*, p. 43) inclines to think that Polycarp thought both quotations from the Old Testament, or else quotes them both as Scripture when in reality only one of them was.

citations, all the phrases are interwoven into the text of the epistle without any sign of conscious quotation. Westcott's judgment that "it is wholly unreasonable to doubt that he was acquainted with the chief parts of our canon" is a safe one.[2] It is true that mere acquaintance does not argue authority. But if we consider his remarks about Paul's letters in chapter 3 we must admit that for all practical purposes (whether theoretically acknowledged or not) the apostolic writings stood alongside the Old Testament as his authoritative source of faith and morals.

In that third chapter Polycarp indicates that when Paul was among the Philippians he taught accurately and stedfastly the word of truth; when he was absent he wrote letters to them "from the study of which you will be able to build yourselves up into the faith given you." To argue from this statement that Polycarp intended two parallel sources of apostolic teaching, one oral and the other written, will not do because only the letters are mentioned as a source of building oneself in the faith. In the face of such evidence for his use of the apostolic writings it is extremely perplexing why Flesseman-Van Leer should say, "there is no clear proof that Polycarp accepts any New Testament Scriptural authority."[3]

Rule of Faith

Only one complex passage in our study of Polycarp remains: chapter 7:1-2. Here the aged writer says that whoever does not confess that Christ has come in the flesh and that he died on the cross "is of the devil." And whoever perverts the oracles of the Lord for his own lusts and says that there is neither resurrection nor judgment is "the firstborn of Satan. Wherefore, leaving the foolishness of the crowd, and their false teaching, let us turn back to the word which was delivered to us in the beginning."

Obviously Polycarp believed that certain doctrines determined one's "orthodoxy." He mentions the incarnation of Christ, his death, the resurrection, and judgment, but more

---

[2] Westcott, *History of Canon*, p. 37.
[3] Flesseman-Van Leer, *op. cit.*, p. 44. Much depends upon the question of formal and conscious recognition of New Testament authority. Submission in fact to the apostolic writings can not be doubted.

important than which particular teachings are listed is the fact that there was a body of such doctrines. Later writers of the second century will call such a corpus of tenets "the rule of faith."

A more troublesome feature of this passage, and in some respects the heart of the problem, is the meaning of *methodeuēi ta logia*. Lightfoot says that it means perverse interpretations of the *logia*, which Polycarp combats by an appeal to tradition.[4] Flesseman-Van Leer, on the other hand, judges that Polycarp meant "to speak in manifest contradiction to the *logia*."[5] This means that when Polycarp calls the Christians back to original doctrine it is not a matter of writings in contrast to tradition but of heretical teaching versus the real tradition of the church.

The problem is complicated by the fact that this use of *methodeuēi* is unique in New Testament and early Christian literature. However, we have seen in our study of Clement of Rome that *logia*, regardless of other connotations, is nearly always associated with the Scriptures.[6] That there is a close association here is suggested by Polycarp's use of "firstborn of Satan." According to Irenaeus, Polycarp on a later occasion applied this title to the heretic Marcion, who mutilated the Scriptures by reducing the number of canonical books and by teaching perverse doctrines (*A.H.* III, 3,4). Since the title comes here in a context dealing with doctrine, Polycarp must mean that the teaching of Scripture is being twisted to yield doctrines contrary "to the word which was delivered" in the beginning. Because "that which was delivered" (*paradothenta*) can be used of either written or oral teaching (II Thess. 2:15), we cannot be sure how this teaching originated. It does seem, however, that Polycarp uses "from the beginning" to contrast apostolic teaching with heretical. The argument is not unlike the one used later by the North African lawyer Tertullian in his *Prescription Against Heretics*.

---

[4] Lightfoot, *Apostolic Fathers*, 5 vols., Part II, II, 2, 919.
[5] Flesseman-Van Leer, *op. cit.*, pp. 46-47.
[6] See B. B. Warfield's study "The Oracles of God" in *Inspiration and Authority of Scripture*.

Creed

Apostolic teaching had not yet distilled into a creed, but, like Ignatius' writings, Polycarp's letter does contain brief creedlike statements. In chapter two he writes:

> Wherefore . . . serve God in fear . . . believing on him who raised up our Lord Jesus Christ from the dead and gave him glory and a throne on his right hand, to whom all things in heaven and earth are subject, whom all breath serves, who is coming as Judge of the living and of the dead.

The most significant feature of this confession is its composition. "The fact that it is a cento of tags from *I Peter*," writes Kelly, "deserves notice as throwing light on the way in which the body of catechetical tradition was built up."[7]

In summarizing our observations from Polycarp's letter two major features are noteworthy: (1) The aged Bishop was deeply indebted to the apostolic writings, chiefly Paul's, for his view of Christianity. To him they were the means of increasing one's stature in faith (3:2). That direct quotations are infrequent in his letter does not of itself mean that he was ignorant of the apostolic books. On the contrary, the way he uses them to express his own thoughts indicates how much a part of his own thinking they had become. (2) Basically from these writings the Bishop drew a number of doctrines that he associated with Christianity. To deny them was in his mind heresy and unbelief. Thus, while he did not employ the term "rule" (*kanōn*), he did appeal to a number of doctrines as later Christian writers (Irenaeus, Tertullian) do to the rule of faith.

Before leaving the Bishop of Smyrna this seems like the appropriate place to append what little information we can glean from the *Martyrdom of Polycarp*. This letter, an "obviously genuine and contemporary account of the martyrdom of Polycarp," was sent by the congregation of Smyrna to the Church of Philomelium shortly after Polycarp's death.[8] Though it is intensely interesting as the first post-biblical

---

[7] J. N. D. Kelly, *Early Christian Creeds*, p. 70. See I Peter 1:21; 3:22; 4:5.

[8] K. Lake (ed.), *Apostolic Fathers*, II, 309.

narrative of a Christian martyrdom, it yields little that will add to our study.

According to the narrative the knowledge of God comes through Jesus Christ (14:1) and may be taught to others (10:1). This is clear from the fact that at one point Polycarp tells a Roman proconsul that he would teach him the doctrine of Christianity if he wished to learn. In addition, Polycarp is three times called "teacher" (12:2; 16:2; 19:1), once with the adjectives "apostolic" and "prophetic" added. Evidently this was a title of esteem, but it is inadequate grounds for uniting the gift of the Spirit and the hierachical office.[9] Finally, there is no doctrine of tradition in the *Martyrdom,* for the one time the verb "deliver" is used it is in the sense of "betray" (1:2).

V. BARNABAS

The document known as the *Epistle of Barnabas* is really an anonymous work and something of a mystery. Aside from the Alexandrian Fathers early notices of it are lacking. Clement of Alexandria thought the author was the companion of Paul, and Origen called it "the catholic *Epistle of Barnabas.*" Because of these references to the work the presumption is that it was written in Alexandria. Certainly the internal style and interpretation evinces an Alexandrian environment. Its date is also something of a problem. J. B. Lightfoot favors A.D. 70-79, but others would place it in the second century. Fortunately these external matters do not blur its internal message.

Scripture

It is evident from the letter that the Old Testament is authoritative. As Bishop Lightfoot has pointed out, the unknown author postulates no opposition between the Old Testament and the New. "On the contrary he sees Christianity everywhere in the Lawgiver and the Prophets, and treats them with a degree of respect which would have satisfied the

---

[9] See Flesseman-Van Leer, *op. cit.,* p. 48, where Abbe G. Bardy is so quoted.

most devout rabbi."[10] He says that the prophets were inspired by Christ (5:6) and therefore could prophesy concerning him. In fact, he attributes the message of the Old Testament directly to God, whether Father, Son, or Spirit (1:7; 9:1-2; 6:14; etc.).

On six occasions he introduces quotes with the formula "the Scripture says."[11] All but one of these refer to the Old Testament, the one exception being to the book of *Enoch* (16:5). This in itself may indicate an Alexandrian milieu, for the Jewish attitude toward the canon was less rigid there than in Palestine. Of the eight other references introduced by "it stands written" (*gegraptai*) only one is in any way unusual. This one precedes the proverbial phrase "many are called but few are chosen" (4:14). This expression is found in Matthew 22:14, but it is possible that Barnabas either did not intend a Scriptural citation or referred to some supposed (rightly or wrongly) Scripture of the Old Testament.[12] Aside from this one possible reference, Barnabas never quotes the apostolic writings, though he is aware of the apostolic ministry of preaching (5:9). This fact, however, is in perfect harmony with the purpose of the book. He is writing to show that the Christian (at least Barnabas) has the true interpretation of the Old Testament.

Basic to that interpretation of the Scriptures is his view of inspiration. When quoting the Old Covenant he uses such phrases as the following: "The Lord says in the Prophet" (Psalm 17:45); "The Spirit of the Lord prophesies" (Psalm 33:13); "Moses spoke in the Spirit"; and "the prophets received their gift from Christ and spoke of Him" (9:1-2; 10:2; 5:6).

Since the Scriptures are thus inspired he can interpret the Law and the history of the Jews "spiritually." He discovers many types of Christ and the cross in the Old Testament (9:14). Most of them are highly fanciful. For example, he finds a prefiguring of the cross in the number of men circumcised by Abraham. While such allegorical interpretation may seem to have the sanction of the canonical book of Hebrews,

[10] Lightfoot, *Apostolic Fathers,* p. 239.
[11] 4:7, 11; 5:4; 6:12; 13:2; 16:5.
[12] Westcott, *op. cit.,* p. 62.

one notable feature is different. In Hebrews the old covenant was real and its ordinances, though not the heavenly things themselves (Heb. 8:7; 10:23), were "patterns of the things in heaven." In *Barnabas,* however, it is assumed throughout that the Law from its first institution was misunderstood by the Jews (14). Fasts and sacrifices were not required in any literal way, only in a spiritual sense (2:3). Circumcision, likewise, was not the seal of God's covenant; it was the work of an evil spirit who induced the Jews to substitute fleshly circumcision for that of the heart (9). In chapter 4:6 Barnabas goes so far as to set up an either/or condition when he denies that the old covenant can be both the Jew's and the Christian's. Commenting on this passage Robert M. Grant rightly observes, "Here Barnabas' typological exegesis leads him to the rejection not only of Old Testament history but also of the general Christian understanding of the meaning of that history."[13]

Gnosis

A problem related to his exegesis of the Old Testament is Barnabas' understanding of *gnosis*. He twice uses *gnosis* to indicate the Christian faith in its widest sense (1:5; 2:3), but at least four other times it designates that truth derived from his christological exegesis.[14] According to Barnabas the propagation of this truth was the first and the only intent of God in the Old Testament revelation. For instance, the regulations concerning food are not to be understood as applying to literal food but must be understood spiritually (10:10). To receive this understanding of Scripture, this *gnosis,* a previous spiritual experience with God is necessary (9:9), an experience that Barnabas calls "the circumcision of ears and heart" (9:3; 10:12).

But when all the supposed mystery is fathomed, this *gnosis* still comes from God through the apostles and Christian teachers (5:9; 8:3). In fact, Barnabas himself is doing nothing else than passing on this *gnosis* (19:1). Evidently he found no contradiction in asserting that God was the source

---

[13] R. M. Grant, *The Bible in the Church,* p. 46.
[14] 6:9; 9:8; 10:10; 13:7.

of this knowledge and in affirming the need for Christian apostles and teachers. In this he anticipated Clement of Alexandria, who said that the Christian *gnostic* tradition may be learned in the prophets as Christ himself taught the apostles during his presence (*Miscellanies* VI, 7). Also like Clement, Barnabas conceived of a spiritual elite who had more knowledge than others in the church (17:2), but this does not mean that only those with *gnosis* are in the church. Was he not writing to pass on truth necessary for salvation (17:1)? Obviously he expected more than the elite to read his epistle.

VI. THE SHEPHERD OF HERMAS

Hermas, the author of the *Shepherd,* tells us that he had been sold into slavery in his early years and then sent to Rome, where he was purchased by a certain Rhoda (*Vis.* 1:1). His brother seems to have been Pius, Bishop of Rome (c. 140-150). Other than this the author of the *Shepherd* remains mysterious.

His book is an apocalypse consisting of twenty-seven tractates — five *Visions,* twelve *Mandates,* and ten *Similitudes.* It belongs very likely to the early second century if not to an even earlier time. We do know that it was highly regarded in the early church. Irenaeus, Tertullian, Clement of Alexandria, and Origen either cite it as Scripture or assign to it special authority. And it was included in at least one early New Testament manuscript.[15]

Christ and the Apostles

Since the author himself claims to have a direct revelation from God, he naturally recognizes God as the formal and final authority.[16] He frequently mentions God's commandments. Christ, he says, received them from the Father (*Sim.* V, 6, 3) and delivered them in turn to the apostles, who preached the message to the whole world (*Sim.* IX, 17, 1). Finally, the responsibility of "proclaiming the word of the Lord" was shared by "teachers" (*Sim.* IX, 25, 2). The result

---

[15] See F. L. Cross, *Early Christian Fathers,* pp. 23-24 and Lightfoot, *op. cit.,* pp. 293-294.
[16] The fifth vision is titled *apokalupsis.*

was a unified faith and love (*Sim.* IX, 17, 4). Hermas, therefore, was familiar with the common body of Christian teaching. He simply felt an attraction for ethical matters and proceeded to emphasize the moral precepts of the gospel.

Whatever his revelations might have been they were not secret tradition. He is reminded repeatedly that his message should be explained to all (*Vis.* III, 8, 10; *Sim.* X, 4, 1). Moreover, a false prophet is recognized for just this reason: he gives his prophecies secretly and to only a few (*Mand.* XI, 13). Such strange doctrines corrupt the servants of God (*Sim.* VIII, 6, 5), especially those who have sinned. Thus, in spite of his fondness of private revelations, Hermas "is nowhere at variance with the general Christian teaching or tradition."[17] The question is, Just what was that teaching according to Hermas?

Creed

In the first *Mandate* the Shepherd commands, "First of all believe that God is one, who made all things and perfected them, and made all things to be out of that which was not." Since Hermas knew the triad Father, Son and Holy Spirit (*Sim,* V, 6, 2), Kelly suggests that this "first of all" began an early catechetical instruction based upon a trinitarian confession.[18] The evidence, however, should not be pressed too far. If this is true, it is the only glimpse of a creed in Hermas, even though baptism does not escape his interest.[19]

Scripture

Hermas is equally silent about the Scriptures. Unlike most of the other Apostolic Fathers, he has no definite reference to either the Old or the New Testament. On the single occasion (*Vis.* II, 3, 4) when he uses "it stands written" (*gegraptai*) he refers to an apocryphal work titled *The Book of Eldad and Modat*. However, though no direct quotations

---

[17] Flesseman-Van Leer, *op. cit.,* p. 60. Cf. *Vis.* III, 3, 2: "And no longer trouble me about revelation for these revelations are finished, for they have been fulfilled."
[18] Kelly, *op. cit.,* p. 67.
[19] This seems to be the meaning of "seal" in *Sim.* II, 17, 4.

are made from the Bible, passing coincidences of language occur throughout the book.

Similarly, the only reference to inspiration in the book concerns early prophets like those mentioned in the *Didache* (*Mand.* XI, 7). Hermas receives certain standards for discerning the true prophet from the false. The true prophet (1) is meek and upright, (2) speaks only when God wishes him to speak, and (3) speaks plainly. Hermas is exhorted to use these criteria and to "test . . . from his life and deeds, the man who says that he is inspired" (*Mand.* XI, 16).

The Holy Spirit also speaks to Hermas but in the form of the church (*Sim.* IX, 1, 1). The church appears to him as a woman and as a tower being built upon water (*Vis.* III,3,5). The water symbolizes baptism. The stones of the tower are the apostles, bishops, teachers, and deacons of the church. Thus the office of bishop is known to Hermas but his chief function seems to be caring for the poor (*Vis.* III, 5, 1; *Sim.* IX, 27, 2) rather than teaching doctrine.

To sum up, Hermas is in many respects unique in the literature of the Apostolic Fathers. Though his positive contribution to our study is minimal, it is of striking importance that he does not present teaching that is radically at variance with what we are able to draw from other witnesses of the same period. Like them he recognizes the revelation of God brought by Jesus Christ and proclaimed by the apostles. If he shows an interest in the dynamic phases of early Christianity — revelations, prophecy, etc. — these do not supersede the ordinary church channels but are communicated through them (*Vis.* II, 4, 3).

VII. II CLEMENT

The so-called *Second Epistle of Clement* is neither from Clement nor is it an epistle. Because it was found immediately following Clement's letter in some of the early manuscripts it came to be ascribed to Clement. This view was held as early as the fifth century. But the internal evidence, its style and doctrine, indicates that it is from another author. As to who he might be we are left to speculation. The writing itself also reveals that it is not a letter at all but a homily that may be dated somewhere around the middle of the second century.

The Teaching

Since it is a homily we would expect the unknown author to recognize the importance of teaching the Christian message. And he does. He exhorts his listeners to give heed to the Lord's commands not only before the presbyters but at home as well (17:3). As to the source of that teaching we learn nothing. When he mentions the church (14) he has in mind the ideal spiritual church "created before the sun and moon." And though he does say that the heathen hear the *logia* from "our" mouth (13:3), he is referring to Christians in general, not only church officials.

Scripture

The chief value of the work is the light it throws upon the author's view of the Scriptures. Four times he uses the word "Scripture" to introduce a quotation (2:4; 6:8; 14:1-2). Three of these clearly refer to Old Testament passages. These, added to chapter seventeen where the author uses "the Lord said" before quoting Isaiah 66:18, are sufficient to show that in the author's mind the Old Testament was authoritative.[20] The question is, Did he conceive of certain Christian works as also "Scripture"? The fourth reference suggests that he did. It is a quotation of Matthew 9:13 and would lead us to the conclusion that certain of the Christian writings were regarded as "Scripture" (II Pet. 3:15-16) before they were collected and looked upon as the "New Testament."

That is not to say that these writings were the sole record of the teachings of the Lord. Usually "II Clement" introduces the words of Jesus with the lemma "the Lord says," and at least three times he employs quotations from apocryphal sources after such an introduction. This simply shows that enthusiasm for the words of Christ superseded the concern for trustworthy sources. It in no way subtracts from the place held by the writings of the apostles. The inconspicu-

---

[20] 17:4. There is a reference to "the prophetic word" in 11:2 which is unknown. Several other O.T. quotes are introduced by "He says." Cf. 2:2; 3:5.

ous way that he introduces expressions from Paul, James, and John shows that their works had become part of his way of thinking. And on one occasion he definitely links the apostles with the Old Testament when he speaks of "the Books and the Apostles" (14:2).[21] Throughout his sermon the way the author of II Clement handles his sources evinces an interest in written rather than in oral tradition.

In short, his fundamental authority was the words of the Lord Jesus Christ (or sometimes God). He found these in the Old Testament Scriptures (13:2) and in the written Gospels. If at times he appealed to other sources as well, it was because he found no just cause for not using them when he thought they might yield the words of the Lord. His action was taken in the face of the growing practice of designating the apostolic writings as "Scripture."

VIII. PAPIAS

Upon Eusebius' testimony we learn that Papias, Bishop of Hierapolis, was a disciple of the "presbyter John" and a contemporary of Polycarp (*E.H.* III, 36 and 39). Whether we ought to understand this "presbyter John" as the apostle John or another man is still very much debated. We also learn from Eusebius that Papias took great interest in the evangelic traditions current in the church, and embodied his research in five books entitled *An Exposition of Oracles of the Lord*. There is no lost work whose recovery would be of more interest to Patristic scholars.

Tradition and Scripture

In one of Papias' surviving fragments he tells us that he carried on his work assuming that "what was to be derived from books would not profit [him] as much as what came from living and abiding voices." This statement, some feel, shows the priority of oral tradition over written authority in the early church. This, however, is not Papias' intent. That

---

[21] An otherwise unknown reference to a saying of the Lord (8:5) not in our Gospels is likely a variant reading of Luke 16:11; another (9:11) may either be a free rendition of Matthew 12:50 or from an apocryphal source.

he lived in days when it was still possible to learn details of the life of Christ from living tradition is unquestioned. But that these oral reports were more important than written Gospels finds no support from Papias.

The title of his work (note: *of Oracles,* not *of the Oracles*) indicates that, while Papias made no claim to completeness, "the oracles" were basic to his research. His "interpretations" presuppose the oracles. Consequently, the oral traditions that he mentioned served only a secondary purpose, to elaborate by way of comment upon the oracles. He himself says that he placed the traditions "side by side" with the interpretations. And the apologetic tone in the description of his writings, indicates that "his reference to tradition might seem unnecessary to some, and that it was in fact only a secondary object."[22]

A more basic issue is, What did he mean by "oracles"? The best way to determine that is to observe how he used the word elsewhere. Fortunately, in the few fragments of his writings that survive he uses the term two other times. He tells us first that Mark became Peter's interpreter and wrote accurately all that he remembered of Jesus' deeds and words. Mark himself had not heard the Lord, but he followed Peter, who used to deliver the teaching but did not make any arrangement of the Lord's oracles (*logiōn*). Second, Papias says that Matthew collected the oracles (*ta logia*) in "the Hebrew language." By "oracles," then, Papias evidently means the actual words of the Lord given during his lifetime. These were obviously oral at first, but that Papias could find these in written Gospels is evinced by his own testimony concerning Gospels by Mark and Matthew.

There is, therefore, no need to hold that Papias included the written Gospels within his reference to "books." In fact, he emphasizes Mark's accuracy in writing the things said and done by the Lord. Certainly from the testimony of other sources there is evidence that Papias believed in "the divine inspiration" of the Revelation (very likely the source of his belief in a millennium).[23] If he viewed the Revelation so

---

[22] Westcott, *op. cit.,* p. 72.
[23] Andreas of Caesarea, *Preface to Apocalypse,* in Lightfoot, *op. cit.,* p. 520.

highly, is there not an *a fortiori* argument (in view of his great interest in the oracles of the Lord) in favor of his acceptance of the Gospels as authentic sources of the oracles of the Lord?

IX. SUMMARY

Just as the question of guilt or innocence at a trial turns upon the evidence produced, so the problem of heresy or Christian truth turns upon the basis of authority. Implicit standards of truth become explicit as they are challenged. About the middle of the second century Marcion and the Gnostics were presenting their case for Christianity so successfully that Catholics were pressed hard to speak in their own defense. For the first time the church was forced to take the stand and give an explicit testimony concerning the foundation of her faith. The Apostolic Fathers are important witnesses to the early Christian view of authority for just this reason: they precede the period of controversy and reveal what was assumed regarding the sources of Christian truth prior to the great trial.

For these early Christian writers God had revealed himself preeminently in and through Jesus of Nazareth. Christ was the supreme teacher of divine truth. This knowledge of the will of God was immediately accessible, however, through the prophets, who foretold the details of Christ's mission, and through the apostles, who had been first-hand witnesses of his life and teaching. This appeal to the two-fold testimony of the Old Testament and the apostles of Jesus is characteristic of this age. When Polycarp called the Philippians to follow Christ along with "the apostles who preached the gospel to us and the prophets who announced our Lord's coming in advance," he was reflecting the attitude of a generation of Christians (*Phil.* 6:3).

The church's submission to the Old Testament as a doctrinal norm in this age is only a projection of the attitude taken by the preceding one. Christ, as the New Testament makes clear, was the key to understanding the Old Testament. Jesus himself led his disciples to this view of the old covenant (Luke 24:44-48). The apostles followed his lead by preaching a gospel that was "according to the Scriptures" (I Cor.

15:3-4). The Apostolic Fathers merely confirm the universality of this practice in the early church. Barnabas goes a bit beyond his contemporaries when he denies that the old covenant belongs to the Jew at all (4:6), but within a few years Justin was to follow the same line of argument in his apology (I *Apol.* 32:2).

This "Christian" view of the Old Testament is of course not on the surface of the old covenant itself. Luke indicates that Jesus "opened the understanding" of the apostles in order to show them this truth. How did the early believers arrive at such a view? They followed, whether consciously or unconsciously, a certain method of interpretation. They read the Old Testament through eyes enlightened by the Christian gospel. Barnabas admits as much when he speaks of his christocentric *gnōsis*. Clement of Alexandria was to do the same later.

How much we are permitted to follow the Apostolic Fathers in this treatment of the Old Testament is not important at this moment. What is significant is that this christocentric view of the old covenant probably preserved the Old Testament for the Christian church when within a few years Marcion tried to expunge it from the Christian corpus of writings.

The parallel doctrinal norm among these writers was the testimony of the apostles. Though the theological importance of the fact is not always evident, the apostles are the channels of God's truth for the church. "The apostles," wrote Clement, "received the gospel for us from the Lord Jesus Christ" (42:1). And, according to Hermas, Christ was preached by the apostles throughout the whole earth (*Sim.* 9, 17, 1).

As B. B. Williams well says, there was among these men no conception of the church as a "legal institution in which the twelve were thought of as the only medium whereby grace or commission could be handed on."[24] The importance of the Twelve as a link with the historic Christ became more urgent with the passing of the years. For the Apostolic Fathers it is enough to recognize the moral superiority of the apostolic men. Ignatius contrasts his captivity to the position

---

[24] B. B. Williams, *Authority in the Apostolic Age*, p. 59.

of the apostles (*Rom.* 4:3, *Trall.* 3:3). Polycarp with deep admiration refers to the wisdom of Paul and his Letter to the Philippians as the foundation stone of their faith (*Phil.* 3:2). And Clement points the Corinthians to Paul's letter, which was written "in the Spirit," and places himself in the same arena as those in Corinth (7:1). Furthermore, the number of citations from apostolic writings is inexplicable apart from this esteem for them shared by all of the Apostolic Fathers. The evidence is more than sufficient to support the claim that "the Apostolic Fathers do separate the writings of Apostles from their own and disclaim apostolic authority."[25]

To suppose that this respect for the apostolic testimony was confined to written documents, however, would be unwise. The Apostolic Fathers drew no sharp line between written and oral authorities. But is this not what one would expect of those within one generation of the apostles? The things that they had seen and heard were still quite real to them. Papias' ready acceptance of authentic oral reports of "the elders" is understandable. Furthermore, of the many citations of apostolic testimony there are few, if any, that are quoted as though the author were conscious of quoting a written authority. The form of the quotation would argue as convincingly that they were derived from oral tradition. It is most probable that the writers had in mind that body of facts and doctrines which found expression in the churches' day-to-day preaching, instruction, and worship. At the same time it must be understood that no quotation contains any truth that is not substantially preserved in our Gospels and Epistles. There is no place for tradition not vouched for in those books later known as the New Testament.

The exclusive authority of the apostolic writings was delayed by several circumstances in the early second century. First, while memory was still fresh there would be no great demand for written records. Second, to the degree that Christ and the gospel could be found in the Old Testament the priority of the apostolic documents would be delayed. Third, since the writings of the Fathers were usually for purposes of exhortation rather than for theological controversy they would

[25] J. F. Bethune-Baker, *Introduction to the Early History of Christian Doctrine*, p. 45.

be less likely to appeal to the apostolic writings for authority. The heresies confuted by Ignatius — Docetic and Judaistic tendencies — were not of the type to call forth a theory of apostolic authority. Marcionism and Gnosticism will do that in the next generation.

The use of the apostolic records for purposes other than doctrinal authority is another matter. There is abundant evidence to show that the practice of the church of this period was to resort to the apostolic writings for edification, instruction, and worship. The freedom with which the writers weave quotations from the apostolic documents into their own indicates a familiarity that transcends any legal relationship. If at times writings and traditions from other than apostolic sources were used, this was due to an inability to foresee the consequences of this practice. Within a generation the church would in practice reject the apocryphal gospels and distinguish between apostolic tradition and ecclesiastical tradition, subordinating the latter to the former. But until challenged to make such a decision, Christians did not always hesitate before quoting a source that would promote the knowledge of the Lord.

Unlike Scripture, tradition in the sense of the authoritative handing down of doctrine or the doctrine so handed down is all but absent in the Apostolic Fathers. Clement's reference to "the rule of our tradition" (7:2) was a rare possible exception. But we saw that this proved to be more ethical than doctrinal. Neither is there any reason to believe that the Apostolic Fathers used a formal creed. J.N.D. Kelly's judgment is a fair one, "There is no suggestion, much less explicit mention of a formal, official creed anywhere . . . On the other hand, there is an abundance of quasi-credal scraps which show that the creed-making impulses of the Christian communities were alive and active."[26] The impulse, which would in time produce creeds, did draw out the implications of the primitive *kerygma*.

Similarly no "rule of faith" as such is mentioned but brief doctrinal statements are to be found. For examples, Polycarp rejects as "the first-born of Satan" anyone who denies the

[26] Kelly, *op. cit.*, pp. 65-66.

incarnation, the cross, the resurrection, and judgment (*Phil.* 7:1); Ignatius stresses the revelation of "one God, who manifested himself through Jesus Christ" (*Mag.* 8:2); and a large portion of the homily of *II Clement* is concerned with the resurrection of the flesh. Like the New Testament there is here no indication as to the extent of this body of doctrine, nor is there any suggestion as to how this "rule" is related to the Old Testament and the apostolic testimony. The evidence simply reveals an awareness that Christian truth is one thing; heresy is quite another.

Finally, any theory of the ministry as an authoritative norm is only hinted. Clement implies that the successors of the apostles inherited the gospel message (42) and *II Clement* urges strict obedience to the elders on the grounds that they are commissioned to preach the faith (17). But, other than passing references, there is faint mention of the ministry as a factor in the pattern of authority.

IV

THE MID-SECOND CENTURY: THE APOLOGISTS

THE EARLIEST CHRISTIAN WRITINGS WERE WRITTEN FOR THE use of believers. As Christianity spread it met with an ever-mounting hostility. This condition called forth a new type of Christian literature. "The Apologists" (in the sense of defenders) is a name given to that group of writers whose common purpose was to answer the pagan accusations against the new religion and to present an introduction to the Christian faith and life. Christianity was at first an exclusive religion. Those who joined "the fellowship" were expected to break cleanly with the pagan syncretistic culture that surrounded the church. Christian exclusivism produced pagan ignorance; ignorance fathered misrepresentation. Three charges brought against the disciples of Christ became common: atheism, infanticide, and incest. Drawing from the best elements of pagan culture the Apologists tried to demonstrate the injustices of the unbeliever's indictment and to gain a fair hearing for the Christian gospel.

Since their writings are addressed to the pagan (often to an emperor), the Apologists try to present Christianity in its most favorable light. No attempt is made to explain the faith fully. The internal worship and teaching of the church are introduced only insofar as information will dispel ignorance and reduce hostility. We should not expect, then, any systematic or developed pattern of authority. The Apologists were seeking to win the favor of an angry public, not to catechize it.

In their endeavor these champions of the faith employed the Scriptures freely because one of the trusted arguments for the truthfulness of Christianity was the one from fulfilled prophecies. The case was strengthened by two other arguments: the one from the seniority of Christianity (that it was temporally prior to the pagan philosophies) and the one from the high morality of the new religion's adherents. Thus the Apologists assumed the task of demonstrating the congruity of the Christian message with the highest ethical and philosophical ideals in the pagan world.

I. QUADRATUS

The earliest Apologist of whom we have any knowledge is Quadratus. Eusebius tells us that he addressed a treatise to the Emperor Hadrian (117-138) because some men were troubling the Christians (*E.H.* IV,3). Though Eusebius had a copy of this treatise we have only a few lines. These are not of great value for our purposes other than to show that the argument from living witnesses as a means of establishing the reality of the works of the Savior was still in vogue. Eusebius also preserves a tradition that Quadratus was distinguished for his prophetic powers (*E.H.* III,37; V,17). This might be a testimony to the continuing belief of the early church in the ministry of the Holy Spirit through chosen men, much as we noted in the *Didache*.

II. ARISTIDES

Along with Quadratus, Eusebius mentions a certain Aristides who also addressed an *Apology* to Hadrian. For many years this work, like that of Quadratus, was little more than a name. In 1889, however, J. Rendel Harris found a Syriac translation of it on Mount Sinai. It was recognized by J.

Armitage Robinson as extant in the Greek in the work known as *Lives of Barlaam and Josaphat*. This latter work is a Christian adaptation of the life of Buddha. The two forms of Aristides' work differ widely, and it is disputed which is nearer the original.

The first part of the work deals with belief in God (on a natural-theology level) and with the absurdity of pagan religions. It is not particularly important for our purposes. However, in the last three chapters (15-17) Aristides gives an appealing description of the Christian life. The description of the high morality maintained by believers is presented to the Emperor as an indication that the Christian has the truth and worships the true God (15). The truth consists of dogmatic and ethical teaching; the faith is derived from the incarnation of Jesus Christ, God's Son. After his death at the hands of the Jews his twelve disciples went forth into the known world and taught of his greatness. Those in Aristides' own day who believe the apostles' message or who keep their doctrine are Christians.

The Scriptures

But how can this teaching be ascertained in Aristides' time? The Emperor is urged to take the Christian writings and examine them. He will learn of the God who is Maker of heaven and earth and of the commandments that are engraved on the mind of the Christian (15,3). Aristides has read these Scriptures and has believed them (16,3). Once, if the Syriac text can be trusted, the Apologist uses the phrase "it is written in the Scriptures" (16,5). Usually, however, he points to these writings simply as a means of introducing the pagan to Christianity, rather than as authoritative documents.

There is one reference to the gospel in the *Apology*.[1] Aristides says that the incarnation and virgin birth of Christ are taught in that gospel which only a short time ago was preached "wherein if ye [the Emperor] also will read, ye will comprehend the power that is upon it." If the Syriac text can

---

[1] Ch. 2 in J. Rendel Harris's translation of the Syriac. J. Rendel Harris and J. Armitage Robinson, *The Apology of Aristidas* in *Texts and Studies*, I, 1, 6-17.

be trusted again, this passage shows that there is an inherent power that validates the truth being presented. While we cannot press the point, this may well reflect Aristides' own view of the Scriptures, a view that included their inspiration and/or the accompanying testimony of the Holy Spirit.

There are no direct quotations from the New Testament in this work but "the Apologist's diction is undoubtedly coloured at times by the language of the Apostolic writers."[2] Harris has shown the similarities in diction and the marked resemblances of phrases, especially to the Epistle to the Romans.

Creed

His attempt to find a "symbol of faith" in Aristides is less convincing, however. As Kelly points out, one misconceives Aristides' argument if one draws a phrase from the theological discussion of chapter one and then several other phrases from chapter two, which deals with traditional christological teaching.[3]

Summarizing, we note that Aristides had knowledge of a body of writings from which he could learn the events of the incarnation and the apostolic teaching. The character of his letter precludes any developed doctrine of Scripture, but the comments one finds in no way conflict with other available information from his time.

III. JUSTIN

Of all the Apologists, Justin called "the martyr" is the best known to us largely because his works are more complete than any other of this period. In these he relates the major facts about himself (*Dial.* 2-7). Born of Greek parents in Samaria, he drifted westward, settling first at Ephesus where he passed through the various philosophical schools of that day: Stoic Pythagorean, and Platonic. None, however, satisfied his thirsty mind. Finally he met an aged stranger beside the sea who instructed him to find the true philosophy in the Hebrew prophets and in the gospel of Christ. He soon became a

[2] *Ibid.*, p. 82.
[3] Kelly, *Early Christian Creeds*, p. 76.

Christian. From Ephesus Justin moved on to Rome, where he taught as a Christian philosopher in the time of Antonius Pius. His days were ended abruptly by martyrdom about A.D. 165. From his pen two *Apologies* addressed to the Emperor and a *Dialogue* with Trypho the Jew have survived the centuries.

The Scriptures

Justin draws his doctrine from the teaching of Christ and from the prophets who preceded him (I *Apol.* 23,1; *Dial.* 134,1). To him this meant that he was not following mere human doctrines but divine teaching, the truth itself (*Dial.* 48,4; 80,3). Had not these writings led him to God? By "the prophets" the Apologist clearly intended the whole Old Testament, because Moses, representing the Law, and Daniel, representing the Writings, are included among "the prophets." In this submission to the Old Testament he is merely following the universal Christian practice. But the way in which he relates Christ to this authority of the Old Testament is a bit unusual. According to Justin, Christ, as the pre-incarnate Logos, taught the prophets (I *Apol.* 63,14). Therefore, to say "the Scripture says" is equivalent to saying "the Logos says" (*Dial.* 19,6; 68,5). And to Justin "the Logos" was Christ.

The teaching of Christ was also accessible in what Justin called "the memoirs of the Apostles." Theoretically these were not yet on a par with the Old Testament but practically they were above it. He quotes the prophets as authority; he uses the memoirs to show that he is not relating fables concerning Christian beliefs and practices (I *Apol.* 14,4). The difference is understandable if we consider his readers and his purpose in writing.

How apologetic considerations determine the use of authorities may be seen in his contrasting use of the prophets in the *Apology* and in the *Dialogue*. For the pagan reader it is necessary in the *Apology* to introduce the prophets (I *Apol.* 31,1) and to explain that the Christian believes these writings because he sees the fulfillment of predicted events (I *Apol.* 30). Such evidence of divine approval induces belief in the prophets as heralds of Christian truth (I *Apol.* 30; 31,7). No such procedure is necessary in the *Dialogue.* Trypho, being a Jew, already accepts the prophecies as true. To show that the prophecies are fulfilled in Christ and in Christian teaching or practice is enough (*Dial.* 110; 117). We must, however, understand this difference as a pedagogical device, not as a difference in belief or thought, because Justin's greatest appeal to the inspiration of the prophets is made in the *Apology.*

Apostolic Writings

As with the prophets, so also with the New Testament, Justin is mindful of apologetic values. Having his readers in mind, he does not quote the New Testament as authority. "He wishes merely to give a true representation of the doctrines and precepts of the gospel," John Kaye writes, "and for this purpose it was sufficient to express the meaning without any scrupulous regard to verbal accuracy."[4] This in no way suggests Justin's depreciation of the New Testament. He tells us that the apostles were sent by Christ to teach (I *Apol.* 39,3), that they and their followers have put this teaching in writing (*Dial.* 103,8), and that these writings are joined with the prophets in Christian public worship (I *Apol.* 67,3). By his own day "gospel" was used to designate these writings (I *Apol.* 66,3; *Dial.* 100,1).

On occasion Justin even goes beyond this. He tends to look upon these "memoirs" as authoritative in their own right when he repeatedly quotes the words of Jesus from them. Once in speaking to Trypho he recognizes a difference in Christ's teaching and the record of it, but he makes no distinction in their authority (*Dial.* 49,5). Westcott's judgment on the importance of the apostolic writings for Justin is that "The written records were now regarded as the sufficient and complete source of knowledge with regard to the facts of the Gospel. Tradition . . . was by Justin definitely cast aside as a new source of information."[5]

Some have raised the question, Does Justin intend our present Gospels when he uses "memoirs of the apostles"? The

[4] John Kaye, *First Apology of Justin Martyr,* p. 108.
[5] Westcott, *History of Canon,* p. 112.

inquiry is worth pursuing because in some details his quotations often do not correspond to our New Testament. For example, he mentions fire on the Jordan at Jesus' baptism (*Dial.* 88) and gives quotations of Jesus not found in our Gospels (*Dial.* 35; 47). Attempting to answer the question, Westcott and Kaye scrutinize the materials. Both answer in the affirmative. Certain details (as the fire on the Jordan) can be explained as Justin's own interpretation, and quotations like Acts 20:35 may be drawn from oral tradition.[6] Other deviations from the Gospels can either be attributed to Justin's fallible memory or to the use of a different manuscript.[7]

In summary, Justin's use of Scripture was largely dictated by apologetic considerations. His "apology" rested heavily upon the argument from fulfilled prophecy. The Old Testament, therefore, carried a major share of his pattern of authority. He used the apostolic writings to prove the truthfulness of his account of Christianity. If it did not seem wise to quote them authoritatively, there is no sufficient reason to question their practical authority within the church. That the books not exclusively written by the apostles would be included under apostolic authority is shown by Justin's ascription "the apostles and those who follow them," which precedes the quotation of a text in Luke.[8]

Inspiration

The authority of the Scriptures rests upon their inspiration by God. In his first *Apology* Justin either states directly or implies that the voice behind and validating the words of the Old Testament writers is the prophetic Spirit. The prophets spoke and were filled with the divine Spirit (*Dial.* 7,1). Their utterances were not their own but those of the Logos, who moved them. That such inspiration extends to the whole Old Testament is shown in the fact that Moses, representing the Law (I *Apol.* 44,1), and David, representing the Writings (I *Apol.* 35,5; 40,5), spoke as the prophets did. Behind the Old Testament, then, there is one Author (I *Apol.* 36,2).

---

[6] Kaye, *op. cit.*, pp. 108-110.
[7] Westcott, *op. cit.*, p. 151.
[8] *Dial.* 103 on Luke 22:44.

While Justin's primary emphasis is upon the prophetic writings, there are intimations that the same inspiration of the Spirit extended to the Apostles (*Dial.* 48,4; 119,6; I *Apol.* 67,3). They too were instruments for God's message. The Apologist does not explicitly discuss the particular mode of the Spirit's inspiration. One word he does use to describe the inspiration is *theophorountai* (literally, "borne of a god": I *Apol.* 33,9; 35,3). In itself this would designate one wholly under the influence of a deity. But apparently even when the prophet was under the Spirit's power his personality remained to some degree, since Justin frequently quotes the Old Testament as the words of the prophet.

Interpretation

His view of the interpretation of Scripture follows from his teaching on inspiration. Since Christ, who is the Logos, speaks both in the Old Testament and in Christian teaching, the two must essentially agree. Justin, therefore, finds "many revelations veiled in parables and mysteries" (*Dial.* 68). He claims that the ordinances of Moses contain numerous types and symbols realized in the Messiah (*Dial.* 42,4). The twelve bells that hung around the robe of the high priest prefigured the twelve apostles (*Dial.* 42,1). The Paschal lamb was a type of the death of Christ (*Dial.* 40,1), even as the offering of fine flour in the case of leprosy was a remembrance of his passion in the eucharist (*Dial.* 41,1). He likewise finds significance in the objects and events of the Old Testament. For example, he sees the symbol of the cross in the tree of life, in the brazen serpent, and in Moses as he stood victorious over Amalek (*Dial.* 86; 90; 91).

The Jews, unable to see that Christ is the message of the Old Testament, cannot really understand it (I *Apol.* 31,5; 36,3; *Dial.* 9,1). Their rejection of Jesus as the Christ is proof enough for Justin that they do not believe the prophets either (*Dial.* 136,3). Did not Christ open the Scriptures and teach the apostles the true meaning of the prophecies (I *Apol.* 50,12; 32,2)? The Old and "New" Testaments are therefore mutually dependent. As Christ explains the prophecies, so they proclaim him. Since the Jews so completely miss this meaning of the Old Testament, the Scriptures cannot rightfully be said to be theirs but are the Christians' (*Dial.* 29,2). One can easily see that this christological exegesis of the Old Testament could go to extremes. It shows little regard for the historic nature of God's redeeming acts. We ought to add in Justin's defense, however, that he never seems to deny the literal truth of the narratives that furnish him with these divine analogies. He was simply convinced that the old covenant and the new formed one harmonious whole. If he met an apparent contradiction he would rather admit his ignorance of its meaning than concede a possible contradiction in God's revelation (*Dial.* 65,2; 115).

Any proper understanding of Scripture, however, demanded the grace of God (*Dial.* 92,1). The prophetic message cannot be understood by just anyone; a man must receive the wisdom from God and from Christ (*Dial.* 7,3). This "grace" is a means of escaping the judgment of God as well as of understanding the Scriptures (*Dial.* 58,1; 119,1). It seems to have some relation to doctrine since in the *Dialogue* the power to understand the prophets is closely related to the ability to explain the arguments in them (*Dial.* 92; 100,2). In this veiled way Justin was probably telling his non-Christian readers, "if our gospel be hid, it is hid to them that are lost" (II Cor. 4:3). We will examine how doctrine relates to Christian conversion shortly, but the idea of "tradition" naturally precedes this.

Tradition

Justin knows of an apostolic tradition. The verb *paradidonai* occurs twenty-one times in his writings. Seven of these signify pagan teaching and are of no significance for us. The other uses, however, refer to (1) Old Testament events or teachings,[9] (2) "the Word of God" (I *Apol.* 53,6), (3) Christ's teachings and his instructions about the Lord's Supper,[10] (4) the apostles' prophecies concerning Jesus (I *Apol.* 49,5; 66,3), (5) the apostles' writings concerning the Lord's Supper, and (6) Christians' proclamation of the doctrine of the Trinity (I *Apol.* 6,2).

---

[9] I *Apol.* 53,6; 60,4; *Dial.* 41,1; 42,1. The detail mentioned in the latter reference does not occur in Ex. 28:33.
[10] I *Apol.* 66,1; *Dial.* 41,1; 49,3; 69,7; 70,4 (twice); 117,1.

Several observations follow from this information: (1) Scripture both "hands down" and is "handed down" — is both *traditio activa* and *traditio passiva*. (2) Those who "hand down" may be the prophets, Jesus Christ, the apostles, or ordinary Christians, but (3) that which is "handed down" is always equivalent to revelation and is authoritative since it ultimately derives, whether mediately or immediately, from Christ. (4) In none of Justin's uses does "that which is handed down" have the connotation of oral tradition as distinct from written; it is consistently used of Scriptural teaching.

Rule of Faith

Information about a rule of faith in Justin's writings is harder to come by. He believes that Christianity rests upon doctrines that are not mere human opinions but are of God (*Dial.* 80,3). These commands of God (to which a Christian's life must conform, I *Apol.* 16,8; 61,2) are summed up in Christ, the Logos (I *Apol.* 21,1; *Dial.* 11,2). One's personal salvation depends upon believing what "God taught through Christ" (I *Apol.* 19,8). Moreover, the believer is taught through him because the Christian teaching is his teaching.

Christ's teaching comes to others through the apostles. Jesus taught them after his resurrection and they in turn preached to the world (I *Apol.* 50,12; 67,8; 42,4; 53,3). Now Justin and other Christians, just as they were taught, are to pass on these dogmas and the Christian rites of baptism and the eucharist (I *Apol.* 6,2; 61,9; 66,1-3).

Since, according to Justin, personal salvation depends upon receiving these doctrines, the question "How many?" becomes most vital. Justin felt that the number of required dogmas was limited. He tells Trypho that a Jew who wants to become a believer and at the same time observe the Hebrew law will be permitted to remain in communion with Christians. The only criteria for a Christian are belief in (1) a crucified Jesus Christ, the Son of God, who received judgment over all men and in (2) his eternal kingdom (*Dial.* 46,1). It was unnecessary to include faith in God because Justin assumed that Trypho, as a Jew, already so believed. Another passage shows that some doctrines were essential, others nonessential. In discussing the millennium he makes clear that he believes in such an earthly reign of Christ but many other Christians of "pure and pious doctrine" do not. Obviously, then, here was one doctrine that did not determine one's salvation. Other dogmas such as faith in the God of Abraham, Isaac, and Jacob, and in the resurrection of the dead, do not fall in this category (*Dial.* 80). Thus while Justin does not specifically mention a "rule of faith" he does presuppose a body of teachings that constitute the essence of doctrinal Christianity. The number of these may be a bit ambiguous but they seem to cluster around the early *kerygma*. In this regard Justin is quite traditional.

Creed

There are a few allusions to a creed or creeds in Justin's writings. In the first *Apology* he gives a christological statement that, if not actually a confession, is akin to one.[11] Later in the same treatise he gives another statement. This one is a tripartite confession associated with Christian baptism (I *Apol.* 61). The "creed" is evidently stated by the one administering baptism, and if so, it would support J.N.D. Kelly's view that interrogatory confessions prevailed at this time. This is also the first tripartite confession of which we have any evidence. This is especially interesting since Justin probably also knew of a developed christological statement. "It is difficult to resist the conclusion," says Kelly, "that St. Justin knew and, on occasion, had recourse to a developed christological kerygma which already enjoyed a measure of fixity and which was still quite independent of the Trinitarian confessions."[12] That Justin's reproductions of this *kerygma* are not especially colored by his own philosophical theology witnesses to that fixity.

Apostolic Succession

In the light of these developments and the later stress upon "apostolic succession" it is an interesting fact that Justin makes no mention of a succession in the churches. Neither does he give the links by which "tradition" is preserved,

---

[11] See 21,1; 31,7; 42,4; 46,5; also in *Dial.* 63,1; 85,2; 126,1.
[12] Kelly, *op. cit.*, p. 75, but note that Kelly calls it *kerygma*, not confession.

though of course tradition as "original delivery" is often mentioned. More than that, like the other Apologists, he never refers to the church other than to denote all Christians collectively (*Dial.* 42,3; 63,5; 134,3). The only references either to officers or to a hierarchy are the ones in which a president (*proestōs*) is said to lead the congregation (I *Apol.* 65,3; 67,4-5). We cannot prove anything from this silence, however, since these matters, like others, may have been governed by apologetic considerations.

Regardless of such silences Justin has made a great contribution to our understanding of this period. (1) He has shown an acquaintance with the Scriptures, both the Old and the New Testaments. Actually, he considers the two to be one in their proclamation of Christ. Because of their inspiration by the Logos, or the Spirit, they are authoritative for faith and practice. The teaching of the biblical writers is not so much their own as God's. (2) Tradition in the passive sense, i.e., what is passed on, is always the teaching of Scripture. Though certainly aware of some details derived from oral tradition, he uses these only to enhance the picture of Jesus found in the Gospels. He shows no awareness of a category of oral tradition, because he assumes throughout his writings that the Scriptures are a sufficient source of doctrine and practice. (3) There are traces of a creed in his writings, but there is no hint of any teaching that could not be derived from Scripture.

For lack of a more appropriate place we may append here the information concerning inspiration found in the anonymous *Exhortation to the Greeks,* which some attribute to Justin. In chapter eight of this work the writer tells us that the biblical writer was used as an instrument in God's hands, like a harp or lyre, and by this means knowledge of divine things was revealed. Did this author, then, consider the biblical writers to be merely passive instruments? However strictly we may be inclined to interpret the metaphor, one thing we must remember: the tone and quality of the note upon a lyre depend as much on the instrument as upon the hand that plays it.[13] The same writer says elsewhere that

[13] Westcott, *Introduction to Study of Gospels,* p. 409.

through the sacred writers the Spirit taught others who were desirous to learn (*Exhort.* 35). What the Christian teachers taught were doctrinal matters or religious truths (*Exhort.* 8).

IV. TATIAN

Justin had a disciple named Tatian, who also wrote an apologetic work. It was called *Discourse to the Greeks*. Born of pagan parents in Syria, Tatian was educated in Greek rhetoric and philosophy. Like his later teacher Justin, he traveled widely in search of truth. Shortly after the middle of the second century he arrived in Rome, was converted to Christianity, and became a pupil of Justin. So long as Tatian remained under Justin's influence there were apparently no signs of a defection from the faith, but after his master's martyrdom (*c.* 165) he returned to the East, founded a sect, and separated from the church. His sect followed an extreme asceticism, condemning marriage altogether.

Like his teacher, Tatian was "a disciple of the barbarian philosophy," that is, barbarian in the eyes of the Greeks (42,1). He had been a disciple of Christian truth since his conversion when he happened to meet with these "barbaric writings" and through them "to come to the truth" (29). He put faith in these because of

> ... the unpretending cast of the language, the inartificial character of the writers, the foreknowledge displayed of future events, the excellent quality of the precepts, and the declaration of the government of the universe as centered in one Being (29).

Hence, Tatian found these writings too divine (*theioterais*) to be compared with the errors of the Greeks (29).

The Prophets

Tatian considers Moses the founder of the "barbarian wisdom" (31,1) but he believes that the prophets also reveal things otherwise unattainable (20,2). Their "barbarian philosophy" consists of a number of doctrines that do not rest upon the opinion of men but upon the commands of God (35,1; 12; 32). These doctrines must therefore be obeyed as the words of God (30). Fortunately these teachings, ordinarily hidden to the soul (13), have been written down (12,5), and in contrast to the conflicting Greek philosophies these constitute a unified system of thought (32). The Apologist does not employ the Scriptures extensively. He quotes them directly only twice and alludes to John 1:5 once (13).[14] He does not mention Jesus Christ, the apostles, the church, or "tradition" in any sense relevant to our study.

His chief argument is one he probably learned from Justin: Christianity is superior to Greek philosophy because it is chronologically prior. Moses, the founder of the "barbarian wisdom," preceded the Greek philosophers. In fact, they secured their teaching from him (40).

Inspiration

Considering the fact that this argument is his fundamental one, his striking remarks about the inspiration of the prophets are most unusual. "The Spirit of God," he says, "is not with all men, but abiding with some who live justly, and being united with their soul, it proclaimed to all other souls, by prophetic teaching, that which had been hidden" (13). Like his teacher, Tatian had come to Christ through the prophetic power of the Scriptures. That he should have the highest view of their inspiration was only natural.

The position the Gospels had achieved by Tatian's time is evinced in his other important work, the *Diatessaron*. This work was a compilation of Matthew, Mark, Luke, and John into a single continuous narrative. The original text of the work has been lost but it is possible to reconstruct it from surviving sources. The significance of the *Diatessaron* lies in the fact that the four Gospels had by the third quarter of the second century (*c.* 172) already received a certain authority as the record of the words and works of Jesus. It also shows, however, that this authority was not so great that Tatian felt any impropriety in combining the four texts into one.

V. THE LETTER TO DIOGNETUS

In many respects the *Epistle to Diognetus* resembles the *Apology* of Aristides, though its style is more rhetorical. In

---

[14] Ps. 8:5 and John 1:3 in *Discourse* 15 and 19 respectively.

all of extant Christian literature there is no reference to the letter or its author. Internal evidence is our only source of information. Therefore, no one really knows the author, and proposed dates range from the early second century to the early third. A third problem concerns the relationship of chapters eleven and twelve to the rest of the work. Because of the break in the manuscript after chapter ten and the change in style, the last two chapters are generally considered to be from another source. While this is likely, it makes little difference for our purposes. The chapters are apparently quite early and, even though from another author or an early liturgy, they may be considered in our study.

According to the opening lines Diognetus was eager to learn of the Christian religion. In order to inform him of the faith, the author discusses the gods of the heathen (II) and then tells him the differences between Jews and Christians (III-IV). The Christian teaching, the Apologist tells Diognetus, is not some invention of men. It has not come through the exercise of the intellect (V,3) nor by any other means of mortal invention; it has been given by God himself. The Creator was sent to men as a man among men (VII,1-2). As a result of this incarnation, man is able to know of God through faith. Such knowledge would be impossible by any other means (VIII,6).

The same general theme is developed in chapter eleven. God sent the Logos, who was from the beginning. He appeared as new (*kainos*) because this was a new departure in God's dealings with men. Now he is born anew (*neos*) in the hearts of the saints, as though incarnate afresh from age to age. Through the Logos the church is enriched and grace is increased among the saints. Thus the Logos is bestowed upon those who seek, those who do not break the pledges (or bounds) of faith nor transgress the bounds of the Father.

The Apostles

When sent into the world, the Logos was dishonored by the chosen people but was preached by the apostles. The writer speaks of himself as a disciple of the apostles, thus hinting at their unique position (though this cannot be pressed, since he calls them "disciples" also). As a disciple of the apostles he administers that which has been handed down (*ta parado-thenta*) to those like himself. But the revealed things are perceived only by faith. Just what form this "tradition" takes is uncertain. Another intimation of apostolic tradition is found in the phrase "bounds [or "decrees"] of the Fathers." The *horia*, which is used here, is a form related to *horos*, which is used of the formal decrees of bishops and teachers assembled in the synods or councils of a later period. Whether, however, the *horia* in *Diognetus* are written or oral is uncertain.

The Scriptures

Certainly the Apologist was acquainted with the Scriptures. In one reference the fear of the Law, the grace of the Prophets, the faith of the Gospels, the tradition of the apostles, and the grace of the church are brought together (XI,6). That he had in mind written sources is attested by two facts: (1) The Law and the Prophets assuredly mean the Old Testament. (2) The "Gospels" being in the plural cannot indicate simply the *kerygma*. Very likely the "tradition of the apostles" refers to an accepted group of apostolic epistles, because in the following chapter I Corinthians 9:10 is quoted and attributed to "the Apostle" (XII,5).

"The Grace of the Church"

"The grace of the church" is a troublesome phrase because "grace" has a variety of meanings depending upon the given context. Found here with Scripture, it may be the first intimation of "the coordinate authorities of the Bible and the Church, of a written record and a living voice."[15] That this "grace" is personal is the very least that can be said. It exults and can be grieved (XI,7). And in another context it is said to be unfolded and multiplied among the saints through the Logos (XI,5). These combined hints strongly suggest that the Apologist may have had the Spirit of God in mind but for apologetic reasons did not wish to be more specific.

Grace is important in one other connection in the work.

---

[15] Westcott, *op. cit.*, p. 407.

The writer speaks of the "grace of the prophets" (XI,5). Taking into account our other observations concerning the word, "grace" here may imply the inspiration of the prophets by the Spirit. L. B. Radford suggests that this may be the case.[16]

VI. ATHENAGORAS

We know little of Athenagoras, another of the Apologists, beyond what we deduce from the two works from his pen, the *Supplication for the Christians* and *On the Resurrection*. He was by birth an Athenian; by vocation a philosopher. He was very probably connected with the School at Alexandria, as Philip of Sidon indicates. From the introduction to the *Supplication* we learn that the date of his writing was about 177.

The Teaching

The *Supplication* is addressed to the emperors Marcus Aurelius and Commodus. It speaks to the three charges commonly brought against Christians: godlessness (or atheism), eating the flesh of their own children (Thyestean banquets), and intercourse such as Oedipus practiced. Athenagoras asserts that the dogmas to which the Christian gives assent are not man-made but divine and taught by God (*Sup.* 11,1). In contrast to the teaching of the philosophers, which expresses mere human opinion, this truth is based upon God's revelation (*Sup.* 7). The term frequently used to designate the Christian faith is *logos* (*Sup.* 4,2; 9:1; 11,1).

The Scriptures

This teaching, as the Apologist makes clear, is derived from the Scriptures of both the Old and the New Testaments. In following the prophets (i.e., the Old Testament), as a Christian does, one is following the truth, not earthly wisdom (*Sup.* 24,5). But along with the prophets (*Sup.* 9,1-2; 10,3; 12,2), the Christian submits himself to the teaching of the apostolic writings.[17] Three times Athenagoras quotes from the Gos-

---

[16] L. B. Radford, *The Epistle of Diognetus*, note *in loc*.
[17] *Sup.* 11, 1 quotes Matt. 5:44ff. with an addition of Luke 6:28 as those sayings on which a Christian is brought up.

pels with the formula *phēsi,* meaning either "He (Jesus) says" or "it (the Scripture) says."[18] In either case, Jesus' words as recorded in the Gospels are considered authoritative for Christian conduct and doctrine even though they are not quoted authoritatively for the pagan reader. The Apologist does not mention the apostles except, when referring to I Corinthians 15:53, he says, "according to the Apostle" (*Res.* 18). This, however, is sufficient to show that he was aware of the apostles' office and writings. Henry A. Lucks says of Athenagoras' use of Scripture: "In them Athenagoras finds knowledge most certain and impregnable. They are at once the source, criterion, and proof of all truth."[19]

Inspiration

Athenagoras considered Holy Writ to be authoritative chiefly because he believed firmly in its inspiration (*Sup.* 7,2). For example, when quoting Proverbs 8:22 he attributes it to "the prophetic Spirit" (*Sup.* 10,3). Many have pointed to Athenagoras as the prize representative of the ancient's rigid view of inspiration. This is due to the metaphor he uses in describing the Spirit's influence upon the biblical writers (*Sup.* 9):

> I think that you . . . cannot be ignorant of the writings either of Moses or of Isaiah and Jeremiah, and the other prophets, who, lifted in ecstasy [*kata ekstasin*] above the natural operations of their minds by the impulses of the Divine Spirit uttered the things with which they were inspired, the Spirit making use of them as a flute-player breathes into a flute.

One may argue from this quotation, as Flesseman-Van Leer does, that the prophets lost their "ordinary human self-consciousness and became mere instruments of the Spirit."[20] But this seems to be an overstatement of Athenagoras' idea. The term *ekstasis* does not necessarily imply a trance. It may

---

[18] *Sup.* 12,3; 32,1; J. H. Crehen in *Ancient Christian Writers,* XXIII, translates it "Scripture says." This appears legitimate from the fact that Prov. 8:22 is quoted by the same formula, *Sup.* 10,3.
[19] Henry A. Lucks, *The Philosophy of Athenagoras,* p. 33.
[20] Flesseman-Van Leer, *Tradition and Scripture,* p. 91.

mean no more than "abeyance."[21] In the *Supplication* Athenagoras simply says that the Spirit was at work in (*enērgoun*) the prophets (10). True, the metaphor of the flute is a strong one, but even in this figure a place is left for God to work *with* the prophet, as the *sun* of *sunchrēsamenou* indicates.

Taken together the material from Athenagoras does not add significantly to what we have seen in earlier Christian writers. It does, however, strengthen previous conclusions. As do the other Apologists, he resorts to an inspired Scripture for his ethical and doctrinal teaching. And, though he gives no hint of a rule independent of the Bible, he does consider scriptural teaching a system.

VII. THEOPHILUS

Five or six years after Athenagoras wrote his *Supplication*, the three books *To Autolycus* appeared. Eusebius tells us that Theophilus, the author, was the sixth bishop of Antioch after the apostles (*E. H.* IV, 20). Like Justin before him, Theophilus was converted to Christianity by means of sacred Scripture (I,14). He therefore admonishes others to come to these writings reverently, and they too will obtain eternal life, for by keeping these God-given laws and commandments one may be saved (II,27).

The Scriptures

The Scriptures are also given to teach us doctrine and morality (II,34). From them we can learn the truth in contrast to opinion from other sources (II,35). The doctrine taught in them is nothing less than divine teaching. Theophilus constantly appeals to these Scriptures for support of his teaching. In his mind this is sufficient to settle any matter under discussion (II,19). He not only quotes the Old Testament authoritatively but he is also acquainted with the

---

[21] As Crehen translates it (*op. cit.*). Liddell and Scott's *Lexicon* gives four possible meanings: 1) standing aside, 2) distraction of mind, 3) astonishment, 4) trance, ecstasy. Cf. Philo's *On the Special Laws* IV, 49: "the reason withdraws and surrenders its citadel."

works of Paul and Luke, and speaks of John as among the Spirit-bearing men (II,13 & 22).[22]

Inspiration

The Apologist is quite ready to concede the inspiration of any number of religious leaders. The Old Testament prophets were able to foretell events because they were under the influence of the Spirit of God (I,14). The Gospel writers were instruments of the same Spirit (III,12), and evidently Theophilus accepted the inspiration of the Greek Sibyl as well (II,9). Twice he quotes her prophecies alongside those of Old Testament sages to support some assertion (II,31,36). Apparently, however, Sibyl was a special extrabiblical voice instructed by the Holy Spirit, because he ridicules all other so-called sages and prophets for being in error (II,33). The Christian alone possesses the truth! Greek poets may be called upon in support of Christian teaching only because they have borrowed or stolen the truth from the prophets (II,37; III,26).

The particular theory of inspiration that Theophilus held is not as developed as that of Athenagoras, but it is interesting. He thought of the scriptural writer as carried along by the Spirit (*pneumatophoroi*). Thus inspired and made wise by God, he was God-taught, holy and righteous (II,9). In some sense the authors were "contained" (*chōrēsantōn*) by the Spirit (III,17), who came down upon them and spoke through them (II,10). It is, therefore, possible to say that God is speaking when we quote the Old Testament (III,9). And since the ultimate author of all the writings is the Spirit of God (III,12), the Scriptures cannot be contradictory in their various parts (II,35).

The Churches

Only once in *To Autolycus* are the churches mentioned (II, 14). In an extended analogy Theophilus says that the world is as the sea, driven and tempest-tossed by sins. As in the sea there are islands, havens, and harbors, so God has given assemblies (*sunagōgas*) called holy churches, in which the

[22] Rom. and I Cor. are quoted in I, 14.

doctrines of the truth survive. Into these churches flee all who desire to be saved. As there are other islands, rocky and barren, serving only to injure and to wreck the ships, so there are doctrines of error and heresies, which destroy those who approach them. These are not guided by the word of truth.

This very important passage contains the seeds of a full-grown doctrine found in Irenaeus and Tertullian. In Theophilus sound doctrine is the vital issue, as is attested by the fact that the analogy shifts slightly in giving the perilous side of the picture. No assemblies are mentioned here, only false doctrine. Yet like the later writers, Theophilus conceived of the truth as in the churches. The "word of truth" spoken of is definitely comparable to the rule of faith in the later writers. It is that body of doctrines which distinguishes truth from falsehood, Christianity from heresy.

VIII. MINUCIUS FELIX

One other author may be included among the Apologists though he is not of great help for our purposes. Minucius Felix wrote his *Octavius* in Latin. It has a number of affinities to Tertullian's *Apology* and probably should be dated close to the North African's work — somewhere around the close of the second century. The arguments, in the form of a debate, are similar to those found in the earlier Apologists. The argument that pagan philosophers borrowed the truth from the writings of the prophets and the moral superiority of Christianity are prominent. "It is we," says Octavius at one point, "who do not show wisdom in dress but in our hearts, who do not proclaim great things but live them, who are proud of having obtained what philosophers have sought in their utmost efforts but failed to find" (38,6). The work makes only one reference to the Old Testament (33,4). No mention is made of Jesus Christ or of the New Testament. Perhaps Jules Lebreton's remarks are the best summary: "This brilliant *Apology* is . . . only an introduction to the faith and this explains its silences."[23]

[23] Lebreton and Zeiller, *History of the Primitive Church*, p. 583.

IX. SUMMARY

It is now time to draw together these details and to make some observations about the Apologists in general. Perhaps the outstanding feature of this group of writings is their persistent appeal to the Scriptures. Regardless of the reasons or causes behind this phenomenon, the effect is obvious. The general high regard for the Bible is all the more striking when one realizes the wide geographical localities represented by the individual writers: Theophilus in Antioch, Athenagoras in Alexandria, Justin in Rome. How can one avoid the conclusion that, with respect to the Scriptures at least, these writers, though writing as individuals, are reflecting the point of view of the church at large?

This submission to the authority of the sacred Scriptures rests in an implicit belief that these writings were the result of the Spirit of God's activity in and through the biblical writers. Though metaphors and phrases of the various Apologists differ in their attempt to describe this work of inspiration, there is general agreement that the resulting product is equivalent to the words of God himself. On the other hand, aside from Athenagoras' figure of the flute, the Apologists seem to indicate that the prophet cooperated to some extent, at least, in the composition of the Scriptures. References are frequently cited by giving the name of the writer, and sometimes his moral and mental condition is mentioned.[24] We must not suppose, however, that the Apologist had any developed theory of inspiration. There was as yet no conflict demanding such a theory. The Apologist was occupied with another type of controversy, the right of a Christian to exist in a non-Christian world. In this struggle he found the argument from fulfilled prophecy and the appeal to inspired writers handy weapons.

In the defense of his faith the Apologist did not consider it prudent to use the New Testament as he did the Old, but we have no basis for doubting that there were writings of the apostles within the church at this time that were received as authoritative along with the prophets.

[24] Theophilus, *To Autol.* II, 9.

Many more complex questions surround the use of a "rule of faith." Was there any such concept? If so, what was its nature? What was its function? Understandably the Apologists' purpose in writing would not demand a detailed explanation of the Christian faith. This much at least is clear: the Apologists believed that the Scriptures taught a corpus of doctrines that were harmonious and not self-contradictory.

Justin alludes to an interrogatory baptismal confession, but what connection this confession had with the scriptural doctrinal system is not asserted. Justin does indicate that a limited number of doctrines marked off the Christian from the non-Christian (*Dial.* 46,1). Much the same thought can be found in Theophilus (II,14) and in the two chapters appended to the *Letter to Diognetus*. In all likelihood the reason we cannot determine the limits of this "rule" is that there were no such limits for the Apologists. Christians explicitly stated their revealed doctrines only as unbelief challenged the truth.

One last question remains: how was this rule (as we shall call it, even though the Apologists did not) related to the Scriptures? In order to best summarize this we have reserved Eusebius' quotation of and about Dionysius of Corinth (*E.H.* IV,23). Dionysius writing to Soter, Bishop of Rome (c. 170-175), reports that Soter's letter, along with a former one from Clement, is read on the Lord's day. It is implied that the public reading of Christian books was customary, but some are not regarded as of apostolic authority, as the following words show. Some heresies were at work. Leaders of the heresies tried to corrupt Dionysius' letter; whereupon he says, "It is not wonderful then that some have attempted to adulterate the Scriptures of the Lord, when they have formed the design of corrupting those that make no claims to their character." It is evident that these writings, which later formed the New Testament, were separated from other books and that we have one more witness to their unique position in the church at this time.

Following this quotation Eusebius tells us that Dionysius "warred against the heresy of Marcion, and defended the rule of truth." It seems most likely that this rule of truth has reference to that teaching which distinguished Christianity from heresy. It was drawn from Scripture but was found also in the living message of the church. "The Rule of Truth and the Rule of Scripture, . . . mutually imply and support each other."[25]

[25] Westcott, *op. cit.*, p. 194.

V

THE LATE SECOND CENTURY: IRENAEUS AND TERTULLIAN

The Creed and the Rule of Faith

ONLY SLOWLY DID THE SECOND-CENTURY CHURCH SENSE THE growing gap between the fount of revelation, the apostolic age, and itself. Under new circumstances the church was not at first entirely clear about the standards of Christian truth. She assumed rather than asserted. This is not to suggest that she had no norm, for the apostolic writings had survived; it simply means that she did not reflect upon her standards until she was compelled by the movement of events to do so. Serious reflection was called for by the second half of the century.

The Crisis

The first challenge to confront the church came from a businessman with a Christian background who came to Rome about A.D. 140. Though at first financially helpful to the church at the imperial capitol, Marcion soon made known his intellectual doubts concerning the differences he saw between the God of the Old Testament and the God revealed by Jesus Christ. He found irreconcilable characteristics in the two. One was legalistic and vindictive; the other was gracious and loving. Christianity to Marcion was absolutely unique, so much so that the Old Testament had to be rejected. In its place he formed his own "New Testament," consisting of an altered Gospel of Luke and ten epistles of Paul.

Needless to say, most Christians found Marcion and his views dangerous. It is said that Polycarp, the esteemed Bishop of Smyrna, upon meeting Marcion in Rome once said to him, "Do you know me? I know you, you are the firstborn of Satan."[1] But the heretic and his views could not be dismissed simply by cursing him. Churches began to raise the question, Which are the Christian books? When they raised this issue, they were struggling with the problem of the New Testament canon. The fact that the church finally formed a New Testament of her own on a par with the Old Testament has been called by Adolf Harnack "The most important event in the history of the Church." In rejecting Marcion's views the church showed that while Christianity was not to be limited to Judaism it would not cut itself off from its roots in the Jewish Scriptures. By an almost universal use of allegorical interpretation of the Old Testament, Christians found the gospel of Christ promised throughout the Hebrew writings. Therefore, far from discarding the "Old Covenant," Christians looked upon it as a necessary preparation for the full presentation of the "New Covenant."

Marcion's views seemed to spring from an extreme version of Paulinism. The second challenge to face the church issued from very little that was truly Christian. It was satisfied to take Christian names (including "Jesus" and "Christ") and Christian Scriptures into an essentially pagan system. This challenge was Gnosticism, a name deriving from *gnosis* (knowledge) because the Gnostic claimed to know the truth of God. What he actually knew, however, was a philosophical quilt of Greek, Jewish, Persian, and Christian patches. The church historian Philip Schaff once called Gnosticism "a one-sided intellectualism on a dualistic heathen basis." The epithet still has merit.

The seriousness of Gnosticism's threat to Christianity is

---

[1] Irenaeus, *Against Heresies*, III, 3, 4.

revealed in the fact that it regarded man's dilemma as fundamentally an intellectual not a moral problem and therefore denied the incarnation. It pretended to be Christian, however, and by using Christian Scriptures, especially the parables and numbers, a most fanciful interpretation could disguise itself behind a mask of biblical texts. This meant that both the church and Gnosticism appealed to the Scriptures, but derived from them extremely antagonistic views. This created the conflict. If Marcionism raised the question, What are the Scriptures, Gnosticism asked, How shall they be interpreted?

Catholic Spokesmen

Reaction to heresy came from several directions within the church, but two of the most outspoken and effective prosecutors of Gnosticism were Irenaeus, a bishop in Gaul (*c.* 180), and Tertullian, a lawyer is North Africa (*c.* 200). Irenaeus, a native of Smyrna, tells us that as a young man (*c.* 130) he sat at the feet of his Bishop, Polycarp.[2] This gave him a second-hand tie with the apostolic age, a fact that helps to explain his conservativism. At an undetermined date he left Asia Minor for Gaul, where he was to become a churchman of considerable influence. We know that he made at least two trips to Rome to seek solutions to two disturbing controversies. While he was on the first of these missions, the fierce persecution of 177 in Gaul very likely took place. Aged Pothinus, Bishop of Lyons, was martyred and soon afterward Irenaeus succeeded him as Bishop. He had a successful episcopate, especially in extending the Christian witness in Gaul. He also found time to write a long list of books, but only two have survived, the massive *Against Heresies,* and the much briefer *Proof of the Apostolic Preaching.*

Tertullian, born of pagan parents at Carthage, received a good education in legal studies and rhetoric. Making law his profession, he went to Rome. After becoming converted to faith in Christ (*c.* 196), he returned to Carthage, where he gave himself zealously to the propagation of his newly found faith. Writing with the vigor of a new convert he poured out

[2] *Ibid.*

a torrent of words on a variety of subjects. Shortly, however, his zest for the Catholic Church dried up and he was drawn into the rigorous system of morals propagated by the Montanists (c. 207). He died at Carthage some time after 220, apparently still critical of catholic indifference to the work of the Spirit. Before his pen fell silent, however, it had made him the most prolific of the Latin Fathers in pre-Nicene times and the father of the theological vocabulary of Western Christendom.

In their writings both Tertullian and Irenaeus charge the Gnostic with making only a pretense of using Scripture. Actually he twists it out of all recognizable Christian sense. For exhibit A they point to the clear passages of Scripture itself, and for corroborative evidence to the fact that Gnostic teaching fails to correspond to the doctrine preached in those churches established by the apostles. Apostolic teaching, they declare, is accessible for anyone who desires to know the truth.

Thus through two serious crises clarity emerged out of conflict. The church appealed to a "New Testament" to complement the "Old," to simple antiheretical creeds or a "rule of faith," and to the "tradition" within the apostolic churches. Each of these had roots in the first century. Surviving the passing of the apostles were a number of Christian writings, the baptismal confession and the *kerygma*, the earliest evangelistic message. These had once contrasted that which was Christian from that which was pagan. Now, due to the clash with Marcionism and Gnosticism, they were mobilized to oppose that which was catholic (in the sense of antiheretical) to that which was Jewish or heretical. But, serving in this new role as catholic standards of truth, in what sense could they claim to be apostolic?

I. THE APOSTLES' CREED

Was there truly an "apostles' creed"? The fourth-century church believed there was. According to Rufinus, a priest of Aquileia (c. 400), there was a tradition which stated that before the apostles departed upon their mission to the various nations they agreed upon a brief summary of Christian doctrine as a basis of their teaching.³ By the sixth century the belief had taken on added details. A pseudo-Augustinian sermon from that time asserts that each of the Twelve composed one of the twelve articles of the creed.⁴ This explanation of the creed's origin remained the prevailing belief throughout the Middle Ages. Few, however, since the fifteenth-century Italian humanist Lorenzo Valla emphatically denied the apostolic authorship, have accepted the theory as anything more than unrestrained imagination. Though the essential content of the creed is apostolic, the present form developed gradually.

What is now called the Apostles' Creed can be traced in its present form no further back than the eighth century. But several hundred years before this a shorter form had taken shape in what is now called "The Old Roman Creed." When, in the year 340, Marcellus of Ancyra made a profession of faith to a synod at Rome under Bishop Julius I (337-352), he delivered the following:⁵

> I believe in God Almighty
> And in Christ Jesus, his only Son, our Lord
> Who was born of the Holy Spirit and the Virgin Mary
> Who was crucified under Pontius Pilate and was buried
> And the third day rose from the dead
> Who ascended into heaven
> And sitteth on the right hand of the Father
> Whence he cometh to judge the living and the dead.
> And in the Holy Ghost
> The Holy Church
> The remission of sins
> The resurrection of the flesh
> The life everlasting.

The comparatively recent study of a treatise called the *Apostolic Tradition* has thrown open the possibility of an even earlier ancestry of the Western creed. The now recognized author of the work, Hippolytus (c.170-c.236), was a

---

³ Rufinus, *Commentary on the Apostles' Creed*, 2.

⁴ Pseudo-Augustine, *Sermones de Symbole*, 240 (in Hahn, *Bibliothek der Symbole*, p. 50, n. 86). Earliest attestation of this kind is in *Apostolic Constitutions*, VI, 14.

⁵ H. Bettenson (ed.), *Documents of the Christian Church*, p. 34.

controversial figure in Rome of the early third century and the most productive writer of the church in that city in pre-Nicene times. In the *Apostolic Tradition* (XXI) he describes the rite of baptism and the requirements for the catechumens of his day. While given in the form of three questions addressed to the neophyte, the creed used in the Roman baptismal service at about 200 is very similar to the creed attested by Marcellus. Thus the ancestry of the Western creed is probably forced back into the second century. Can it or any other creed be traced any further?

Early in our present century a widely held theory stated that the origin of the Old Roman Creed could be traced to the church's struggle with Marcionism. By identifying the creed with the rule of faith, the proponents of this theory assumed that a fixed declaratory creed existed by the time of Irenaeus and Tertullian, and then proceeded to discover similar forms at an even earlier date. Buttressing the whole endeavor was a view (of Christian origin) that a simple message of love and brotherhood preached by Jesus was converted under Greek influence into a formal theological system.

A new turn in credal studies was taken in the 1920s with the publication of Hans Lietzmann's *"Symbolstudien."* As a consequence the old theory has fallen under searching criticism in recent years and has been shown to lean upon rather meager support. It is now generally agreed that too much weight rested upon two rather thin assumptions: 1) that the rule of faith was identical with the creed at the end of the second century, and 2) that declaratory creeds appeared very early in the service of baptism.

The rule of faith, which does not take definite form until the last quarter of the second century, was akin to a creed only as two distant relatives of a common stock called "apostolic tradition." The old theory argued that the rule of faith was not a fixed expression of the creed because of the Christian policy of withholding the intimacies of the faith from the uninitiated. Such a practice, however, while necessary in the fourth century in order to close the door of the church to those seeking to enter solely for secular advantages, would be purposeless in an age of persecution. Second, evidence for declaratory creeds in the service of baptism before the end of the third century simply does not exist. What do we in fact find in the second century?

Second-Century Confessions

First, we find, in what scholars now call "the prehistory" of the creed, brief creedlike statements. These can be found in the New Testament itself. The confessions "Jesus is Lord" (Rom. 10:9) and "Jesus is Christ" (I John 2:22), probably used in connection with baptism, are the best known, but others can also be found. One in the opening verse of the Gospel of Mark may well be the ultimate source for the fish symbol of early Christian art. The Greek word for fish, *ichthus,* results from taking the initial letter of the words forming the confession "Jesus Christ, Son of God, Savior."

Alongside single propositional formulas like these, we find in the earliest literature two- and three-member statements. The classical example of the two-member type is in I Corinthians 8:6, where "one God" is set alongside "one Lord." The three-member type is best illustrated in the baptismal formula of Matthew 28:19 and in the benediction of II Corinthians 13:14.

These brief statements continue to appear in the Apostolic Fathers and the Apologists. The "Christ-confession" is particularly characteristic of Ignatius, as we have seen, and the triadic formulas are especially prominent in Justin's first *Apology* (chs. 6,13,61,65,67). But all three types appear throughout the second century. A careful study of them discloses two trends: with the passing of the years the single-member "Christ-confessions" tend to merge with the other types and then the triadic formulas become dominant. The reason for the ascendency of the three-member type is likely traceable to the universal practice of baptism in the name of the Father and of the Son and of the Holy Spirit.

Second, we find the earliest confessions of faith associated with the rite of baptism. Eusebius of Caesarea prefaced the creed that he produced at the Council of Nicea (325) by these words: "As we have received from the bishops before us, both in our catechetical training and when we received the baptismal bath . . . so we now believe and bring our faith forward to you."⁶ Evidently by the fourth century the creed in the East served to indoctrinate the catechumen as well as to examine his faith at the time of baptism.

References to the confession in the second century seem to center on the administration of baptism rather than upon the instruction preceding it and on an interrogatory creed rather than a declaratory one. In describing the baptismal rite of his own and probably an earlier day Hippolytus affirms that the presbyter states the creed by addressing three questions to the candidate. After each one the neophyte responds with "I believe."

Much the same practice prevailed elsewhere. At Carthage Tertullian writes in *The Chaplet*, "We are thrice immersed, making a somewhat fuller response than the Lord appointed in the Gospel [that is, the Matthean formula]."⁷ And in his *Resurrection of the Flesh* (ch. 48) he adds that "the soul is bound not by the washing, but by the candidate's answer." One earlier witness, Justin, as well as two later ones, Cyprian and Dionysius of Alexandria concur with this general view of the baptismal service.⁸ Taken collectively the evidence — from Rome, Carthage, Asia Minor, and Alexandria — may be assumed to represent universal practice.

In this connection it is interesting to observe what articles had been added to the trinitarian formula that followed the Lord's command in Matthew 28:19. In Hippolytus' *Apostolic Tradition* the candidate for baptism is asked: Do you believe in God, the Father Almighty? Do you believe in Christ Jesus, the Son of God? (Then a lengthy christological statement follows including Christ's virgin birth, crucifixion under Pilate, death, resurrection, ascension, and coming again.) Do you believe in the Holy Ghost, and the holy church, and the resurrection of the flesh?⁹ This structure of the creed clearly echoes the early trinitarian formula, but by A.D.

---

⁶ Cited by Athanasius in Appendix to *Defence of the Nicene Council*.

⁷ Ch. 3. So in *On Baptism* he says, "A man is lowered into the water and dipped *with intervals for a few words* . . ." (ch. 2, italics ours). See also ch. 13 and *Against Praxeas* 26.

⁸ See Kelly, *Early Christian Creeds*, pp. 40-49.

⁹ B. S. Easton, *The Apostolic Tradition of Hippolytus*, pp. 46-47 (sec. 21) or G. Dix, *The Apostolic Tradition*, p. 33.

200 the affirmations concerning the church and the resurrection of the flesh had been added.

Tertullian, probably representing a slightly earlier period, almost apologizes about the addition of the article on the church. After a candidate confesses his faith in the Father, Son, and Holy Spirit, "a mention of the church is necessarily added," he says (*On Baptism* 6). His defensive tone suggests that the addition of the article did not pass unopposed.

What motives lay behind these added articles no one can with certainty say. We do know that profession of the necessary articles at baptism ushered the believer into Christ's fellowship, the church. And it was out of this general context — the admission of neophytes into the church — that the later creeds were most likely formulated. Though delivered four decades ago Lietzmann's conclusion still seems safe: "It is indisputable that the root of all creeds is the formula of belief pronounced by the baptizand, or pronounced in his hearing and assented to by him, before his baptism."[10]

Third, we find several short declaratory formulas coming out of settings where the faith is challenged. The first is the short summary of Christian belief given to the prefect Rusticus by Justin at his trial.[11] "Our worship," Justin confesses,

> is given to the God of the Christians, Whom we believe to have been at the beginning the sole maker of these things, and the author of the whole world, and to the Son of God, Jesus Christ, Who has also been announced by the prophets as destined to come as a herald of salvation to the race of men and as a teacher of noble doctrine.

The second is the confession in the so-called *Letter of the Apostles*.[12] A pseudonymous treatise, it is probably to be assigned to Asia Minor some time after the middle of the second century. The text professes faith

---

[10] *Die Anfänge des Glaubensbekenntnisses*, p. 226, quoted in Kelly, *op. cit.*, p. 30.

[11] See E. C. E. Owen, *Some Authentic Acts of the Early Martyrs*, p. 49.

[12] Hans Lietzmann, *Zeitschrift für die Neutestamentliche Wissenschaft*, XX (1921), 173ff.

In God, the Father Almighty;
In Jesus Christ, our Savior;
And in the Spirit, the Holy, the Paraclete;
Holy Church;
Forgiveness of sins.

As it stands it appears to be modeled upon the threefold interrogation employed at baptism with the added clauses tacked on the end. But in claiming to be the creed of "Great Christianity" it mirrors the catholic controversy with Gnosticism. Evidently the Gnostics, finding the creeds of value, were parodying catholic formulas. This, at any rate, seems to be clear from the creed of the heretic Marcus found in Irenaeus' great work *Against Heresies*.[13]

The third brief confession is the one produced by the bishops at Smyrna who found Noetus guilty of heresy (*c*.180).[14] Formulated as it is in the context of Noetus' overstress upon the unity of the Godhead (monarchianism), it witnesses to the growing importance of fixed confessions as weapons against heresy.

Fourth, even more obviously a sword forged for doctrinal conflict is the "rule of faith" that we meet in the writings of Irenaeus and Tertullian. Because of its particular role in the whole problem of authority we have reserved a separate treatment for it. However, before turning to that study perhaps a summary of the results of our investigation of the creed would be in order.

Summary

The original function of the confession was to distinguish Christian from non-Christian in the rite of baptism, not to separate catholic from heretic. The older theory, which saw the earliest creed as purely a polemical weapon, has failed to meet the test of evidence. Since post-Nicene creeds were used as tests of orthodoxy and since these creeds were de-

[13] See F. J. Badcock, *History of the Creeds*, p. 28. Principal Lindsay in *The Church and the Ministry* (p. 222) reconstructs the creed of the Gnostic Apelles.
[14] It comes to us in two slightly differing forms in Hippolytus' *Noetus* I and in Epiphanius' *Refutation* LVII. The two may be compared in Badcock, *op. cit.*, p. 35.

claratory ones polemically worded, naturally the question of the early appearances of declaratory creeds is introduced. The older theory that such formulas could be traced back into the second century has failed to withstand further examination of the facts. Moreover, the slow rate of standardization of the creed runs contrary to what one would expect if the creed was fashioned from the heat of the battle with heresy. Third, those holding to the old theory once thought that the extensive christological article in the rule of faith argued in favor of the use of the creed for polemical purposes. Recent study has shown, however, that this extended statement concerning Christ can be explained by the incorporation of articles from the early *kerygma*.

All of this is not to contest the fact that the early confession did become a sword of the Spirit in the battle for truth. We know that the early creedlike statements were so used. And evidence seems to indicate that, when heresy seriously threatened, the church did not hesitate to employ those weapons she had earlier forged for her own domestic purposes. Among these was the baptismal confession.

Considering the whole problem of authority, the final question about creeds must be, From what source or sources was the confession drawn? By the fourth century most Christians believed that the creed was drawn from the Scriptures. Marcellus, introducing his creed sent to Bishop Julius, says that he had been taught the creed "out of the Holy Scriptures."[15] At the same time Cyril of Jerusalem in the catechetical instruction to his church exhorts, "Expect to find every article of the creed proved by Holy Scripture." The creed, he says, is "like a tiny grain of mustard seed, holding all the divine contents of knowledge in the Old and in the New Testament."[16]

While the writers of the second century would not deny such assertions, they had a greater confidence in their ability to search out the apostolic testimony even apart from Holy Writ. The question of the sources for the second-century creed directs us to a more comprehensive problem, the role of tradition in the second-century scheme of authority. However,

[15] Epiphanius, *Ref.* LXXII, 2.
[16] *The Catechetical Lectures* V, 12.

before turning to this we should first understand the meaning and the use of the rule of faith.

II. THE RULE OF FAITH

The phrase "rule of faith" has become a part of Protestant vocabulary through the oft-used affirmation of belief in the Bible as the rule of faith and practice. This direct identity of the Bible with "the rule of faith" fails to gain the unqualified endorsement of the early church. While in no sense intending to oppose the written Word by the spoken Word, early Christians found it necessary to appeal to a series of doctrines under the name "rule of faith," doctrines that could be traced, they thought, to the apostles even apart from their writings.

The word *kanōn* (rule) is used in the New Testament and the Apostolic Fathers of a standard of living or a pattern of conduct (II Cor. 10:13, 15; Gal. 6:16; Phil. 3:16; *I Clement* 7:2). But toward the end of the second century it is applied to doctrinal norms. By the fourth century it is used of the decisions of councils and, as we have seen, in the special sense of canon of Scripture.

Irenaeus and the Rule

The full significance of the rule as an authoritative norm of doctrinal truth is disclosed in the writings of Irenaeus and Tertullian. Both use the phrase freely. Though the meaning is practically the same as Tertullian's "rule of faith," Irenaeus prefers the expression "rule of truth." Simply "rule" (*kanōn*, or *regula*) will not do. In nearly every case where he uses "rule" (*regula*) alone it refers to some heretical system or doctrine. In the only exception to this practice (*Against Heresies* II, 25, 1-2) we cannot be certain what the Greek original underlying the Latin was. Thus even here his usual policy may have prevailed. Assuredly Irenaeus employed the phrase "rule of truth" deliberately. The explicative genitive serves to throw "truth" in apposition to "the rule." It might read just as well "the rule, that is, the truth." This is clearly indicated in one context where both "rule" and "truth" are cast side by side as objects of a common verb.

But what precisely does Irenaeus mean by "rule of truth"? In one passage he asserts that the true believer retains in his heart "the rule of truth which he received through baptism" (*A.H.* I,9,4). This comment has led some to identify the rule of truth with the baptismal confession. Other uses of the phrase, however, fail to support this assumption. That a number of his statements of faith are built upon a triadic formula is undoubted, and that he had specific doctrines in mind is unquestioned (*A.H.* I,22,1; III,1,1), but that these dogmas had taken a fixed form cannot be shown. The beliefs are similar to those of the baptismal creed at that time, but the evident flexibility in expressing them would argue against any rigid formulation received at baptism.

The relation of the rule to the Scriptures is an equally troublesome problem. A close affinity is undoubted. In one place the Bishop argues that the Gnostic, who gathers names and expressions from the Scriptures by twisting them out of their natural sense, is like those who advance a fanciful theory and attempt to support it by appropriating texts from Homer. Anyone who knows Homer will immediately recognize the verses but will also know that the quotations are wrenched from the context and applied to an alien subject. Just so, anyone who holds the rule of truth in his heart recognizes the scriptural selections used by the Gnostic but he refuses to acknowledge the blasphemous system constructed by them. The rule of truth is thus closely related to the proper interpretation of the Bible.

In another place Irenaeus writes: "The rule of truth which we hold is that there is one God Almighty. . . ." Then he proceeds to support the dogma by quoting Psalm 33:6 and John 1:3 (*A.H.* I,22,1). Apparently the Bible is the concrete source of the doctrines that make up the rule. This would explain his identifying the rule with the words of God (*A.H.* IV,35,4). Yet to affirm that the "Bible is the rule of faith" would be to say more than Irenaeus himself says. The rule may set the limits beyond which teachers of the Scriptures may not go. It may also itself be extracted from the words of the prophets and apostles. But it is probably best described as the purport of Scripture, the truth of God necessary for salvation and preached in the church (*A.H.* III,15,1; IV,33,7).

Possibly the closest parallel one could find is Paul's use of "gospel." The term is flexible enough to apply equally well to the elemental themes of salvation and to the whole Christian view of God's program of redemption. In I Corinthians 15:1-5 the great apostle uses "gospel" as including Christ's death, burial, resurrection, and appearances. But in Romans 1:16-17, which introduces the whole book of Romans, "gospel" summarizes the thesis of the epistle, "the righteousness of God from faith to faith." Similarly, Irenaeus thought of the rule of truth as that brief summation of Christian teaching (probably based upon a trinitarian framework) imparted to the catechumen. But under the challenge of an elaborate Gnostic system it was an adequate term for the whole revelation of God.

Tertullian and the Rule

Tertullian, who prefers the phrase "rule of faith" over Irenaeus' "rule of truth," sets forth the specific dogmas of the rule on three occasions (*The Prescription* 13, *Against Praxeas* 2, *Veiling of Virgins* 1). In order to illustrate how he employs the rule it may be well to have one of these before us. In *The Veiling of Virgins*, written during his Montanist days, he says:

> There is only one rule of faith, unchangeable and unalterable: that of believing in one only God, omnipotent, the creator of the world; and his Son Jesus Christ, born of the Virgin Mary, crucified under Pontius Pilate: on the third day raised again from the dead; received into heaven; now sitting at the Father's right hand; who will come to judge the living and the dead, through the resurrection also of the flesh.

This statement, the shortest of the three, omits any reference to the Holy Spirit. Why this should be, especially during his Montanist days, is a mystery. Enough is here, however, to make a number of observations.

The mere fact that Tertullian sets forth the faith in this way has led to the suggestion that he is presenting the baptismal creed of that day. Strong evidence, however, would deny any fixity of the rule. It is true that the doctrines listed are much the same, but each of these can be treated so as to oppose some threatening heresy. For example, the article on creation in *The Prescription* 13 asserts that God "produced all things from nothing," a comment which is lacking in the briefer rule given above. The remark is in evident contrast to the Gnostic teaching of a mediate creation.

Nor is the order of doctrines in every case the same. In one instance the article concerning the gift of the Holy Spirit may precede the belief in the second coming of Christ while the reverse may be true in another. Finally, the fact that none of the statements is unusually close to what we know of the baptismal creed at the time would argue against identifying the rule with the creed.

One reason advanced for this identity is Tertullian's assertion that the rule is "unchangeable and unalterable." One might argue that he means by this that Christ handed down a symbol of faith to his disciples and that they in turn transmitted it to succeeding generations in the church. This, however, is not at all a necessary deduction. Tertullian does say that the rule was taught by Christ and that he gave it to the apostles (*Presc.* 13,44) but he seems to think of the truth of God as a series of ideas committed to the church but variously expressed.

Assuredly the doctrines that make up this rule of faith may be found in the Scriptures. In his treatise *Against Marcion* he speaks of the Gospel of Luke being in accord with the rule of the other three Gospels (IV,5). Apparently he intends the teaching found in these writings, teaching which is an integral part of them but not necessarily expressed in precisely the same words as those used by the Evangelists. This comes close to the meaning of Irenaeus' "rule of truth" when he applies it to the proper interpretation of the Bible.

The flexibility in expressing the rule in no way subtracts from its normative character. The body of teachings collectively, and every doctrine separately, are essential to the faith. A heretic is marked by his failure to adhere to this teaching (*Presc.* 3; *Against Hermogenes* 1). Denial of one dogma is grounds for withdrawing the title "Christian" (*Resurrection of the Flesh* 3). Put positively, whoever knows the rule knows all that he needs to know for the faith (*Presc.* 14). In fact, the rule may be taken as a synonym for the faith (*Veiling of Virgins* 1-2), since the revelation of God brought by Jesus Christ and the faith of the church are for all practical purposes the same.

In the end, Tertullian's rule differs very little from Irenaeus' rule of truth. It appears to be a body of doctrines immanent in the revelation brought by Jesus Christ and expressed in the message of the apostles whether written or oral. It is a set of ideas more than a series of words. It provides the boundaries of Christianity. Within it there is freedom for inquiry and investigation (*Presc.* 12,14), but one step outside these limits excludes one from Christianity because "faith has been deposited in the rule, it has a law, and in the observance of it is salvation" (*Presc.* 14).

VI

THE LATE SECOND CENTURY: IRENAEUS AND TERTULLIAN

Tradition and Scripture

THE COMBINED INFLUENCE OF MARCIONISM, THE GNOSTIC sects, and Montanism upon the church in the latter half of the second century resulted in two important developments: Christian writings that could boast an apostolic origin were elevated to a position of supreme authority and the church's living tradition of apostolic testimony (*paradosis*) became a vital weapon in defense of the truth. At the time these two norms, Scripture and tradition, were seldom separated in the minds of the faithful. For our purposes, however, it will be necessary to discuss them separately before explaining their relationship to each other.

I. TRADITION

Our previous survey has shown that the word tradition (*paradosis*) was very rarely used in any sense related to Christian doctrine. Justin, who might appear to be a noted exception, does use the idea if not the word (I *Apol.* 45,61), but the only time he uses "to hand over" in connection with the apostles he refers to written Gospel tradition (I *Apol.* 66:3). The birth of the concept in terms significant for authority had to await the crisis created by Marcion and the Gnostic sectaries. Part of the explanation why these groups with their appeal to a secret unwritten tradition posed such a problem for the church springs from the general attitude toward oral tradition in the ancient world.

Tradition in the Ancient World

The Greeks of the ancient world found the written word dead, the spoken word vibrating with life. In his *Phaedrus* (275) Plato (427-347 B.C.) belittles the merits of writing. "For it is like a picture, which can give no answer to a question, and has only a deceitful likeness of a living creature." The great Athenian looked upon knowledge (*epistēmē*) as less a matter of "know *that*" than a matter of "know *how,*" and "know how" could not be communicated through the written page.[1] Hearing rather than reading afforded an opportunity for exchange, cogitation, and learning. In this view he was typical. For the Greek thinker it was the oral, not the written, word that imparted a throb of life.

For the Jew oral teaching served a different purpose but shared a common emphasis. Scribism of New Testament times was marked by a high degree of memorization. Instruction consisted of a tireless and continuous exercise of the memory. The pupil had only two duties. One was to keep everything faithfully in memory; the other was never to teach anything otherwise than as it had been delivered to him. This is the reason the teaching of Jesus created such a stir; it was with authority, not as the scribes (Mark 1:22). In this way traditions of leading teachers were passed down from one generation to another. Over the years there grew up around the Torah a law of custom called the Halakkah, consisting of developments from the several commands of the Law. By Jesus' time this law of custom was as binding as the written Torah. In fact, according to Schürer, antipathy toward the "appointments of the Scribes" (*sophrim debre*) was a heavier transgression than opposition to the decrees of the

---

[1] See John Gould's *The Development of Plato's Ethics*, ch. 1.

Torah itself.[2] Thus tradition, resulting from the "authentic" exposition of the written Law, became in practice the ultimate authority.

In Alexandria, Greek and Jewish cultures met in Philo, a first-century Jewish writer and thinker who bore the impress of his Greek training and who undoubtedly influenced the church at Alexandria. In his *On the Special Laws* (IV,28) he wrote:

> Customs are written laws, the decisions approved by men of old, not inscribed on monuments nor on leaves of paper which the moth destroys, but on the souls of those who are partners in the same citizenship. For children ought . . . not to despise them because they have been handed down [*hē paradosis*] without written record.

The early church felt the influence of such ideas as these. Her struggle with tradition as a standard of truth was enacted against the backdrop of this respect for the "traditional." "The principle," Moffatt summarizes, "underlying the vogue of oral tradition in general was that, if a practice or belief had a good pedigree, this amounted to a guarantee that the custom must be substantially legitimate. Long descent invested it with authority, and placed it above questioning."[3]

With this conception obtaining, the church faced in the course of the second century an unparalleled challenge of alien teaching. Tradition, which was not at first distinguished from Scripture, came to be differentiated within the church. Marcion's canon hastened the definition of an orthodox New Testament but the Gnostic appeal to an esoteric tradition not only added to the urgency of this task but called forth an authentic tradition of exegesis as well. The writings of Irenaeus and Tertullian both reflect and help to create these developments.

Irenaeus on Tradition

The standard ancient work against the Gnostics' case for a secret tradition and the only source of much of our knowledge

---

[2] E. Schürer, *The Jewish People in the Time of Jesus Christ*, II, 1, 324ff.

[3] James Moffatt, *The Thrill of Tradition*, p. 20.

of second-century unbelief is Irenaeus' *Against Heresies*. Written a short time before A.D. 188, the opus contains five books in which Irenaeus tries to show that the Gnostics' esoteric teaching is contrary to the message of the apostles. If anyone wants to know what Jesus Christ taught he can readily find it either in the written Scriptures or in the public proclamation of the churches established by the apostles (*A.H.* III,1,1). This divine truth, irrespective of its form, is what Irenaeus calls "tradition."

This can be shown simply by tracing the word (*paradosis, traditio*) through his works. *Against Heresies* contains thirty uses of the noun and at least fourteen instances of the verb. Examining them we find that either the apostles or the churches (sometimes presbyters) may "hand down" the true faith. And the tradition itself is contained both in the Scriptures and in the public preaching of the apostolic churches. No clear distinction is maintained between written and oral testimony. That tradition can refer to the Scriptures, however, is plain in at least one instance. In Book III, 21,3 the catholic apologist argues that the apostles are in full accord with the Septuagint translation of the Old Testament and vice versa. He mentions Peter, John, Matthew, and Paul by name. The inclusion of Matthew makes it clear that if he did not think exclusively of the Gospels he certainly had them in mind. In other places public preaching is just as clearly in view. Thus judging from his use of *traditio,* the way in which the message of the apostles has been preserved is only of secondary interest to Irenaeus. His great concern was to show that Gnostic secret tradition was not the doctrine of the apostles. This was the turning point of the contest.

The Gnostic claimed that a secret tradition was necessary in order to understand Scripture. At one important point in his tome this argument launches Irenaeus on his most extensive treatment of tradition. In this one passage, Book III, 1-5, he clearly has in mind the Christian message preached in the catholic churches rather than the written message of Scripture. In this lone instance the Gnostic sects' claim to a secret tradition forces him to fight them on their own ground, oral tradition, in order that he "might cut off their retreat" from Scripture.

As this passage shows, in his conflict with heresy without question the Bishop's fundamental weapon is the Bible. He says, "When they are refuted from Scriptures" — as though this were his first line of attack — "they turn around and accuse these same Scriptures, as if they were not correct, nor of authority . . ." (*A.H.* III,2,1). Only after this onslaught from Holy Writ is evaded does Irenaeus advance his argument based upon the apostolic message preserved in the churches by successions of bishops. Then, once he disposes of this defense of the Gnostic, he reverts to his argument from Scripture. Flesseman-Van Leer, recognizing Irenaeus' basic argument, affirms that "the entire book *Adverses Hereses* is, broadly speaking, but a 'demonstration from scripture' that the church doctrine is right and the Gnostic doctrine false."[4]

Irenaeus on Succession

However, because Book III, 3, which stresses episcopal succession, has been the center of much debate it deserves extensive quotation here. Irenaeus writes:

> Those who wish to discern the truth may observe the apostolic tradition made manifest in every church throughout the world. We can enumerate those who were appointed bishops in the churches and their successors down to our own times; who neither taught nor knew anything like what these heretics rave about. . . . Since however it would be very tedious . . . to enumerate the successions in all the churches, we confound all those who in any way . . . hold unauthorized meetings. This we do by pointing to the apostolic tradition and the faith that is preached to men, which has come down to us through the succession of bishops; the tradition and creed of the greatest, the most ancient Church, the Church known to all men, which was founded and set up at Rome by the two most glorious apostles, Peter and Paul. For with this Church, because of its position of leadership and authority, must needs agree every church, that is, the faithful everywhere; for in her the apostolic tradition has always been preserved by the faithful from all parts.

---

[4] Flesseman-Van Leer, *Tradition and Scripture*, p. 130. See in this regard *Against Heresies* II, 35, 2; III, 19, 2; and IV, 34, 15.

The great churchman then proceeds to list the Roman bishops beginning with Linus and ending with Eleutherus (174-189), the twelfth, in his own day.

Without entering the controversy over this passage beyond what is necessary for our purposes, certain observations are in order: 1) Like the New Testament (Acts 20:17, 28) Irenaeus makes no clear distinction in this context between bishop (*episkopos*) and elder (*presbuteros*).[5] If, as is often assumed Irenaeus is here supporting a succession of bishops that he considers necessary for the existence of the true church, that succession must be conceived in terms broader than is frequently done.

2) The leader of the flock at Lyons is confident that he can trace a succession in other churches just as he does in Rome. The Church of Smyrna, where Polycarp was appointed by the apostles, and the Church in Ephesus, founded by Paul and taught by John, are also true witnesses to the tradition of the apostles. This is not to suggest that Irenaeus' selection of the Church at Rome as the example was purely arbitrary. On the contrary, she had a "preeminent authority." This authority was based on the fact that Rome was the imperial capital and on the historical facts of the Church's founding.[6] Unlike any other church, she was established by *two* apostles, the two most prominent, Peter and Paul. Thus, Irenaeus argues from historical, not from dogmatic, grounds as the Roman Catholic Church does today.

[5] *Ibid.*, III, 2, 2: *successiones presbyterorum* (see also *Proof*, ch. 3); III, 3, 1: *episcopi in Ecclesiis*. Though we must recognize two offices from another passage (III, 14, 2), Irenaeus in Eusebius, *E.H.*, V, 24, 14, mentions Anicetus, Pius, Hyginus, Telesphorus, and Xystus as *presbyters* before Soter. The reconciliation of these two features offered by Lightfoot is that the episcopate was created out of the presbytery and at this time both titles could be used of the same person. This view has great merit. Lightfoot, "The Christian Ministry," *Philippians*, pp. 227-228.

[6] "*Ad hanc enim Ecclesiam propter potiorem principalitatem necesse est omnem convenire Ecclesiam.*" *A.H.*, III, 3, 2. The translation is highly controversial. Morton Enslin suggests with W. L. Knox that Irenaeus may be reflecting the widespread view in antiquity that in Rome, to which all roads led, was of necessity to be found a cross-section of all life and thought, even primitive doctrine. "Irenaeus: Mostly Prolegomena," *Harv. Theo. Rev.*, XL (July, 1947), 159, n. 67. See also B. H. Streeter, *The Primitive Church*, pp. 65ff.

3) It is likewise significant that Irenaeus does not identify the apostolate and the episcopate. His list of successive bishops (or presbyters) does not begin with the apostles, Peter and/or Paul, but with Linus, to whom the care of the church was first entrusted. Only later, "when the bishop was conceived as the successor of the Apostles in a deeper and more mystical sense," was the apostle drawn into the list.[7]

In summary then, tradition is for Irenaeus the truth of God delivered by Jesus Christ to the apostles. In his time it was the Christian faith and the truth of Scripture. It is an appropriate norm of Scriptural interpretation and may at times be considered synonymous with the *kerygma,* since the barbarian races without the written Word have salvation written in their hearts by the Spirit. These, too, can be said to have the tradition (*A.H.* III, 4,2).

Apart from the Scriptures, the best way of demonstrating the fact that the catholic churches possess this tradition is to point to successions of bishops in those churches established by the apostles. If we resort to such, these citadels of truth will prove the catholic right and the Gnostic wrong, but they are only a means to this end. Irenaeus is a witness to episcopal succession only in a sense that will take into account the observations we have made above.

Tertullian on Tradition

Though much like Irenaeus in his general appeal to tradition as that message delivered to the churches by the apostles, Tertullian shows a development beyond his predecessor. Unlike those before him, the North African after his conversion to Montanism used tradition as we do today, to denote that which has been in practice for generations. In this sense we should perhaps speak of "traditions" rather than "the tradition" because he has in mind Christian customs and practices like making the sign of the cross and triple immersion. These have no foundation in Scripture (*Chaplet* 3); they rest only upon human and therefore relative authority. This means that there is every possibility that one such custom

---

[7] H. E. W. Turner, *Pattern of Truth,* p. 330. Protestants who maintain that the Apostles form dogmatically a unique category find support from Irenaeus at this point.

may be contrary to another. For this very reason, Tertullian argues, the Paraclete is needed:

> So long as the Rule of Faith remains fixed, the other succeeding points of discipline and all manner of life admit of novelty and correction through the grace of God to the end . . . the Lord sent the Paraclete precisely because human mediocrity was unable to take in all things at once, in order that discipline should, little by little, be directed, controlled and brought to completion by the Holy Spirit, the Vicar of the Lord.[8]

By this single maneuver Tertullian saves himself the embarrassment of his new Montanist position and distinguishes between what we may call ecclesiastical tradition and apostolic tradition. He allows for development and change, providing the rule of faith remains fixed.[9]

This distinction was an extremely important development, as later church history proves. That an ecclesiastical tradition (chiefly in liturgical practice) existed from the beginning of the church is undoubted and that an indirect influence was exerted upon doctrine seems likely enough. But for the church of the Fathers, Scripture is the criterion by which liturgical practice must be judged. Tradition in this sense cannot be alleged as an authority for anything the written Word rules out. An observance may be established, if not by Scriptural command, then, according to Tertullian, for some good reason (*On Fasting* 10). But if it is contrary to Scripture it must be abandoned.[10]

In his use of apostolic tradition Tertullian, unlike Irenaeus, never speaks as if it were accessible apart from the Christian

[8] *Veiling of Virgins*, 1.
[9] So *The Chaplet* 3. This well may support that distinction to which La Piana points. He indicates that Victor's ruling in the Easter Controversy brought to light the main difference between Hellenistic Christian tendency and the new Latin Christian policy. The former conceived of tradition as something eternal having a divine value in itself, unchangeable even in its smallest details, to be kept under any circumstances. The latter looked at tradition as of relative validity, reserved to the controlling power the right to modify and to reinterpret it in the light of new events and circumstances. "The Roman Church at the End of the Second Century," *Harv. Theo. Rev.*, XVIII (July, 1925), 235.
[10] See F. W. Dillistone and others, *Scripture and Tradition*, pp. 32-38.

writings. In fact, in *Against Marcion* (IV,5), where he is eager to defend the canon against Marcion's mutilations, he uses the term "tradition" solely of Scripture. Elsewhere also the "handing down" of the truth is by means of the "prophets and apostles" (*Against Hermogenes* 45; *Against Praxeas* 13). Even an account of biblical events or specific doctrines might be described as tradition.

In other places, however, he makes plain that the apostolic tradition is also found in the churches of his day (*Against Marcion* I,21). But even here he intends by tradition the voice of Scripture speaking authoritatively within the apostolic churches. Used in the ultimate sense of the authoritative act through which Christian revelation is known, *tradere* is for Tertullian a rich word. It carries a double shade of meaning. It connotes both the identity of that which is today taught in the church with the original revelation, and the continuity of this revelation.[11]

In brief, tradition is for Tertullian the Christian faith and the truth of Scripture. Since it has been handed down from the beginning of the gospel it can be described as evangelical (*Against Praxeas* 2). Since it proceeds from the apostles it is apostolic (*Against Marcion* V,19). And since it is held throughout the church it can be called catholic (*On Monogamy* 2). How does it differ from the rule? Only as the rule is the doctrinal embodiment of the tradition, the distillation of the apostolic preaching.

Tertullian on Succession

Tertullian's classic polemic against heresy, *The Prescription Against Heretics*, contains his most elaborate reference to "apostolic succession." Its argument runs like this: Christ delivered the truth, the true tradition, to the apostles. These men spread this tradition and by preaching founded churches. All churches founded directly by the apostles, plus all churches springing from these churches, are apostolic. The true faith is that which comes through these apostolic assemblies. Heretical teaching is not found in these churches;

---

[11] Flesseman-Van Leer, *op. cit.*, pp. 149-150.

therefore, the heretics must be accounted as false teachers, non-Christian and, therefore, denied the use of Scripture.

In this argument Tertullian is following both apostolic and Roman law procedure. There are New Testament statements showing the worthlessness of discussion of Scripture with convicted heretics (Titus 3:10,11), since they only echo their stock interpretations. They must be brought to the test of the apostolic *praescriptione* — the custom of the churches (I Cor. 11:16). Even more likely, however, in Tertullian's mind was the right, allowed by Roman law to a plaintiff in an action, to limit the inquiry to a single point. The point Tertullian chooses is the legitimacy of the heretics appeal to Holy Scripture. He aims therefore to show reasons why the interpretations of any one outside the church should be dismissed without examination, apart from any consideration of their intrinsic merit. If he can establish this point the heretics are at once ruled out of court, as having no grounds for a case.[12]

This neither means that Tertullian was unwilling to argue individual doctrinal issues — his other works prove this — nor that Holy Writ was for him subordinate to succession. It simply means that for purposes of strategy he emphasizes the agreement of the Scriptures and doctrines derived from them with the faith that descended from the apostles through the apostolic churches. Even while appealing to succession he was thinking of tradition in terms of the Scriptures. This is evinced by his reference to the apostolic churches and especially Rome, which "combines the Law and Prophets with the writings of evangelists and apostles" (*Presc.* 36).

The difference between Irenaeus and Tertullian in this matter of succession is noteworthy. While Irenaeus names individual bishops, Tertullian stresses the succession of apostolic churches.[13] Apparently Tertullian is less concerned with the process of transmission and more with the content of tradition. For both of them, however, the historical succession is primarily a way of laying hold upon the apos-

---

[12] Bethune-Baker, *An Introduction to Early History of Christian Doctrine*, p. 57.
[13] Only in *Presc.* 32 and, in passing, *Against Marcion*, IV, 5 does Tertullian mention the order of bishops explicitly.

tolic tradition.[14] Even Irenaeus' appeal to certain men cannot justifiably be compared to the later practice of quoting the "Fathers," a practice almost unknown in the Church before the fourth century.[15] Irenaeus' technique is much like that of Hegesippus. From Eusebius we learn that Hegesippus, being from the East, took a trip to Rome mingling with many bishops along the way (*E.H.* IV,22). He found the same doctrine among them all. He discovered in each city, including Rome, "things as the law, the prophets, and the Lord preached." Doctrine was his primary concern; making lists of successive bishops was an auxiliary thought.[16] As Hegesippus himself shows, such a succession offered no insurance against false teaching in Jerusalem.

Secret Tradition

A final word about tradition must be devoted to secret tradition. By the fourth century the practice of keeping details of the Christian faith from the non-Christian seems to have obtained. In his preface to the exposition of the creed, Rufinus tells us that it was never written down.[17] Likewise, Cyril of Jerusalem did not quote the creed in detail in his *Lectures* because of the convention that the creed must be kept secret from the uninitiated.[18] This has come to be called the rule of secrecy, and is discussed at length in *Early Christian Creeds* by J.N.D. Kelly.[19] The problem is, Just how early did this practice obtain?

Kattenbusch once argued that this rule of secrecy is the reason that the creed was not written in Tertullian's time. As Kelly points out, however, Tertullian had no hesitation

[14] C. H. Turner, "Apostolic Succession," Swete's *Essays*, p. 129. remarks: "Alike to Irenaeus, to Hegesippus, and to Tertullian, bishops have their place in the apostolic succession only in connection with churches over which they preside."
[15] See Socrates, *Ecclesiastical History*, II, 37.
[16] It is not even certain that "lists of bishops" is the meaning of *diadochēn epoiēsamēn*. See H. E. W. Turner, *op. cit.*, Appended Note E.
[17] Rufinus, *Commentary on the Apostles' Creed*, preface.
[18] Cyril of Jerusalem, *Catechetical Lectures* V, 12.
[19] Pp. 168ff.

about describing the ceremony of baptism.[20] And we have already noted that Irenaeus goes to some length to show that the churches do not, as the Gnostics, withhold or have access to any secret tradition or *gnōsis*. "If the Apostles had known hidden mysteries," he writes, "which they were in the habit of imparting to 'the perfect' apart and privily from the rest, they would have delivered them especially to those to whom they were also committing the churches themselves" (*A.H.* III,3,1). Similarly, Tertullian says that the apostles did not keep back anything from their disciples or the churches (*Presc.* 24). These facts taken collectively seem to support Kelly's conclusion — that this rule of secrecy prevailed from the second half of the third century to the middle of the fifth — not any earlier. Interesting proof of the fact that there was no secret apostolic tradition comes from the fact that those who sought to supplement the four Gospels were unable to use any significant amount of oral tradition left over after the Evangelists had selected their material. On the contrary, they had recourse to mere fiction.

II. THE SCRIPTURES

In its approach to the Scriptures as a doctrinal norm, the church of the second century faced two important questions: What are the Scriptures and how shall they be interpreted? The first deals with canonicity, the second with exegesis. In both instances Irenaeus and Tertullian were significant witnesses. In the case of the history of the canon they represent the close of that age which established the church upon the principle of a canon of Christian writings. In the case of biblical interpretation they present the first developed approach to the problem of tradition and its relation to Holy Writ. Before examining their testimony it will be well to summarize the developments in the history of the canon up to their time.

History of the New Testament Canon

The Bible of the earliest Christians was the Old Testament. Thus the church was never without a Bible. Jesus Christ

[20] Kelly, *Early Christian Creeds*, p. 87.

and his apostles accepted implicitly the words of the Law, the Prophets and the Writings. Quite naturally this attitude was conveyed to the early church. However, the experience of grace and the impact of the Holy Spirit would not permit believers to accept unchanged the inherited Jewish idea of the old covenant. The new covenant, taken over from Jeremiah's prediction (Jer. 31:31-34), incorporated in the Gospels and enacted in the Lord's Supper, was very much alive among Christians. The time had not come when the idea reposed in written documents but as soon as the apostles were linked with the prophets as heralds of Christ the possibility was opened. How soon the apostolic writings became the conscious and natural counterpart of the prophetic Word is not the easiest question to answer.

As we have noted, evidence from the Apostolic Fathers is extremely difficult to evaluate. Traces of most New Testament books are not hard to find, but this alone is insufficient testimony for canonicity. To ask, What books were known? is assuredly not the same as to ask, What degree of authority did these books possess? Of course, much depends upon what one means by "canon." If it means an accepted list of books used in public worship and endowed with authority beyond other books of merit, then most scholars of the subject would consider reference to a New Testament during the first quarter of the second century premature. Practical submission to the "words of the Lord" and the witness of the apostles is another matter. That this existed from the very first is undoubted.

Reverence for the words of Christ helps to explain the early acceptance of the four Gospels as authentic sources of Christian truth. Why there should be four accounts instead of one may have caused some practical problems for a time, and we know that other Gospels were popular in sections of the church, such as the Gospel of Peter at Antioch. But by the middle of the century the four Gospels as we know them were classics. Since Justin speaks of "the memoirs of the Apostles" and quotes from our Gospels, it is certain that he knew Matthew, Mark, and Luke. While evidence of his acquaintance with John is less certain, in view of his apologetic purpose and the production of the *Diatessaron* by his disciple, Tatian, there is little reason to doubt his knowledge of all four. Two decades before the end of the century the Muratorian Canon and Irenaeus consider the canonicity of the four Gospels a closed issue.

The Pauline letters were equally respected within the subapostolic church. The New Testament itself bears ample testimony to the circulation of these letters among the churches (Col. 4:16) and to their early collection (II Peter 3:15-16). Pauline theology in the Apostolic Fathers witnesses to the great apostle's continuing influence. His letters are cited or echoed some sixty times. And in Gnostic circles Basilides (c.120-140) and Valentinus (c.135-160), like II Peter, refer to the Pauline letters as Scripture.[21] Finally, since Marcion's canon consisted largely of Paul's letters they must have been gathered at least by A.D. 145, and a date as early as the end of the first century may be nearer the truth.

Taken collectively the evidence suggests that through liturgical and personal use the Gospels and Paul's letters gradually achieved a recognized status equal to that of the inherited Jewish Scriptures. The Gospel canon was generally accepted at least as early as the years between Justin and Irenaeus (150-180), while the Pauline corpus followed a short time later. In time Acts came to serve as the natural link between the two, and by Irenaeus' day I Peter and I John had joined the other eighteen books. The presence of the Marcionite canon, as students of the subject have pointed out, undoubtedly hastened this process, but it cannot be considered the sole or even the controlling influence. The position these books achieved was the result of a selection within the church governed by an almost unconscious awareness of which books presented the truth of God. To speak of "criteria of canonicity" sounds too official. Once the process was completed the church gave much more specific reasons for her selections than she could have done during the second century. Explicit standards were used, but at a later date and in order to judge a relatively few disputed books. Yet some type of informal basis of judgment unquestionably

---

[21] Hippolytus, *Refutations* VI, 29 and VII, 14. R.P.C. Hanson (*Tradition in The Early Church*, pp. 195-197) suggests that the special authority of the Pauline corpus preceded that of the Gospels.

existed during the early decades of selection. What these were can best be treated after we complete this sketchy history of the canon. The normal desire of human nature for the whole picture and the inferences that can be applied to the earlier period demand this.

According to Eusebius, writing about A.D. 330, the books finding the greatest difficulty in achieving a recognized place in the canon were Hebrews, James, II Peter, II and III John, Jude, and Revelation (*E.H.* III,25,1-5). While Revelation was accepted in the West, it found great difficulty in the East. Hebrews, on the other hand, accepted in the East, was at first rejected in the West because the Latin Church denied that Paul wrote it. Only with the passing of time did the belief that Barnabas was its author fade and Pauline authorship gain acceptance. Revelation likewise won a place in the East. The attitude toward the smaller Catholic Epistles is harder to trace because of their brevity and relatively rare use. But by the end of the fourth century there was no longer any serious dispute over the twenty-seven books that now make up our New Testament. Athanasius, Bishop of Alexandria, listed precisely these books in his famous *Easter Letter* of A.D. 367. And various councils in the West took the same position before the close of the fourth century.

Tests of Canonicity

By what tests were these first books accepted and others rejected? We can only draw certain inferences from later standards applied to disputed books and the evident attitude of the second-century church. At best a large measure of mystery remains.

The basic test was authorship by an apostle or an apostolic man. The reverence for the apostles, manifest in the Apostolic Fathers and in Papias' *Expositions,* may be considered typical of the attitude that would hasten the acceptance of any writing claiming apostolic authorship. Sometimes the claim alone was sufficient; sometimes it was insufficient. Opposition to Hebrews in the West subsided only after supposed Pauline authorship was accepted. On the other hand, the *Didache,* which purports to be the record of apostolic teaching to the Gentiles, won a place for a time in Egypt but was finally rejected by the church at large.

Apostolicity, however, must not be conceived too narrowly. From the beginning certain books, like Mark and Luke, were received that could make no claim to direct apostolic authorship. In these cases it was apparently unnecessary. That Mark wrote for Peter and that Luke was Paul's close companion was enough. In the end, therefore, the test was less that of apostolic authorship than of apostolic content. Also, the inherent worth of the writing itself impressed the Christian consciousness.

The general respect for apostolicity, however, raises the question, What were the grounds for the accepted superiority of the apostles? Was it simply because they were first-hand witnesses of Christ, like so many bystanders at the scene of an accident? Or were they especially endowed with the Holy Spirit for the ministry of preaching and writing for the churches of all ages? Some conservative scholars argue that the controlling test of canonicity was inspiration.[22] But how did one recognize this unless it was assumed in a work by an apostle? While this test can be defended after the event, it fails to account for the acceptance in certain quarters of works that were neither apostolic nor inspired — unless works like *I Clement* were included under the supposed sponsorship of Peter or Paul.

While any canonicity on a par with the Old Testament would normally assume inspiration, we should not think of apostolicity as a clearly conceived standard of canonicity apart from other factors that played a part in the total process. One such consideration was the orthodoxy of the work. Did it conform to or conflict with the message the churches inherited from the apostles? This test would naturally eliminate those works that were clearly heretical Apocrypha. Others, however, which were orthodox enough but non-apostolic, would prove a bit of a problem. This is clear from the presence of works like *II Clement* and *The Shepherd of Hermas* in some biblical manuscripts and lists of canonical books.

[22] R. L. Harris, *Inspiration and Canonicity of the Bible.*

Finally, the relationship between the use of a book in public worship and canonicity is obviously close. One of the steps toward canonicity must have been to secure a place on the reading list of some influential church like Rome or Antioch.[23] The canonical Revelation (1:3) contains specific instructions in this regard; we know from Justin that liturgical reading of Christian books occupied an important place in early Christian worship (*I Apol.* 67); and the Muratorian Fragment comments about the *Apocalypse of Peter*, "some will not have it read in church." That public reading alone did not insure the final acceptance of a book is shown by Clement's letter, which was read before the Corinthians.[24] But if it did not of itself guarantee canonicity it provided, as H.E.W. Turner puts it, "the matrix within which Canonicity took shape."[25]

Such a comment reminds us that we should not think of these so-called tests as mutually exclusive. It was rather a matter of dovetailing and mutually supporting one another. In the end, the internal message of the books themselves centering in Jesus Christ prevailed.

Irenaeus and Tertullian on the Canon

Most of the principles set forth in this short resumé are illustrated in the writings of Irenaeus and Tertullian. The Bishop of Lyons regularly refers to the Scriptures as though the apostolic writings were well defined, fixed and authoritative for doctrine (*A.H.* V,30,1). We have argued above that his fundamental defense of orthodoxy rested in the Scriptures. In outlining his position he says, "it is easy to prove from the very words of the Lord" that the catholic acknowledges one Father and Creator, to take only one doctrine (*A.H.* II, 11, 1). He charges Gnostic teachers with turning from biblical proof and accusing the Scriptures "as if they were not correct, nor of authority" (*A.H.* III, 2, 1). Thus, for Irenaeus the supreme court in matters of doctrine is the Bible.

[23] Streeter, *op. cit.*, pp. 3-23.
[24] Eusebius, *E. H.* III, 16; IV, 23.
[25] H. E. W. Turner, *op. cit.*, p. 253.

Tertullian, like Irenaeus, looks upon the Christian writings as part of the existing canon. In his mind the Scriptures unite the Apostles and Evangelists with the Law and the Prophets (*Presc.* 36). These books so combined are authoritative. From this collection the church at Rome, for example, drinks in her faith (*Presc.* 36). If anything, Tertullian is even more legalistic than Irenaeus in his use of these writings. An example of his attitude is his remark to Hermogenes: "If it is nowhere written, then let it fear the *woe* which impends on all who add to or take away from *the written word.*"[26] Thus the Scriptures constitute the deposit from which Christian teaching is drawn.

Of the heretics' use of the Scriptures he says, "From what other source could they derive arguments concerning the things of faith except from the records of the faith?"[27] The instruments of doctrine, or the means by which doctrine is managed, are differently arranged and corrupted by the heretic, but, Tertullian asks, "What is there in our Scriptures which is contrary to us? ... Of them we have our being..." (*Presc.* 38). Is any other conclusion possible than that Tertullian was insisting upon precise agreement between catholic teaching and the Scriptures, the latter serving as the source and standard of the former?

But which New Testament books were included in Scripture? Irenaeus quotes from the four Gospels, Acts, the Epistles of Paul (with the exception of Philemon), I Peter, I and II John, and Revelation. If we add to these Philemon and III John, which could have been omitted simply because of their size, we would not be far from the New Testament as Irenaeus knew it. Tertullian's canon is much the same. In addition to these he is acquainted with Hebrews, written by, as he believes, Barnabas. In all likelihood he also knew Jude.[28]

---

[26] *Against Hermogenes,* 22 with reference to Rev. 22:18-19.

[27] *Presc.* 14. He indicates in *Resurrection of Flesh* 3 that the heretics' doctrine is really drawn from heathen wisdom. They are unable to support their teaching from the Scripture alone, implying that this should be done.

[28] A. Souter, *The Text and Canon of the New Testament,* pp. 170-174.

Inspiration

These writings shared with the Old Testament the authority inherent in books inspired by the Spirit of God. The general attitude toward their inspiration is expressed in the Muratorian Fragment: "Though various principal ideas are taught in the different books of the Gospels, it makes no difference to the faith of believers, since in all of them all things are declared by one principal (or sovereign) Spirit."[29]

Irenaeus concurs. His *Proof of the Apostolic Preaching* is simply a series of biblical texts gathered to support the "apostolic preaching." In it he habitually attributes the writings to God. "The Holy Spirit says" is his regular mode of speaking of the Scriptures (chs. 2,24,38,42). The same is true in his larger work. The Spirit speaks through the prophets (*A.H.* IV,20,8) and the New Testament writers (*A.H.* III,16,2); as a result, the Scriptures are divine (*A.H.* II,27,1) and perfect (*A.H.* II,28,2). Nor does he fail to explain how the writers were inspired. "It is not man who utters the prophecy, but the Spirit of God, taking form and shape in the likeness of the person concerned, spoke in the prophets." Thus the excessive mechanistic conception of some earlier writers like Athenagoras is not magnified.

Their divine inspiration explains the unity found in the Scriptures. They are, as Irenaeus says, "from one and the same Father" (*A.H.* IV, 10, 1; II, 28, 2). The prophets, speaking as they were moved by the Spirit, were witnesses less to their own day than to the coming of Christ. And the apostles testified to the same Christ though from firsthand experience.

One difference is noteworthy, however. While the one Spirit controlled both Old and New Testament writers, the New Testament inspiration is of a higher (or at least a different) order. Only from the clear revelation of Jesus Christ do the riddles and ambiguities confronting men under the Old Covenant become clear. Christ is the treasure hidden in the Old Testament (*A.H.* IV,26,1), and so the ac-

---

[29] Westcott, *op. cit.*, Appendix C. For Jewish view of inspiration note Josephus' *Antiquities*, IV, 8, 49 and X, 2, 2, where Moses words are considered equivalent to God's.

complishment had to take place before the prophecies became comprehensible.

Tertullian, like Irenaeus, viewed the Scriptures as a product of divine inspiration. In his attribution of the words of a passage he unconsciously slips from the biblical writer to the Holy Spirit and vice versa (*To His Wife* II, 2). And in dealing with one passage that appears to contradict another, he seeks some explanation in harmony with the others, since it is unthinkable that the apostle could contradict himself (*Monog.* 11). The reason for this lies again in the unity supplied by the one ultimate Author — the Spirit of God (*On Patience* 7).

Since God has given this written revelation, it is sufficient for dogmatic purposes that the Scriptures speak (*Against Praxeas* 29). Succinctly put: "What is written cannot but have been" (*Flesh of Christ* 3). Frequently in referring to the Scriptures the North African apologist will use the term *instrumentum* (*Presc.* 38; *Ag. Marc.* IV,2, etc.). W.P. LeSaint feels that this is a result of his training in law and means that the writings have legal value, that is, they confer legal rights on the doctrine they contain.[30] If this is true, as it seems to be, we can understand how his argument turns at times upon the verbal exactness of the text, in fact, upon the difference in a singular and plural form (*Monog.* 4).

Allegorical Interpretation

Such a view of inspiration has decided implications for exegesis. The problem of interpretation of the Scriptures was a particularly disturbing one for the orthodox because of the heretics' allegorical handling of Holy Writ. As Robert M. Grant has shown, the use of allegory was all but universal in the ancient world.[31]

The Greek, who desired to retain some reverence for Homer in the face of emerging forms of ethics, physics, and metaphysics, had to find some means of reconciling the two. His answer lay in the supposed symbolical or hidden meaning of the great epic poet. Stoics in particular used this method

[30] W. P. LeSaint, *Ancient Christian Writers*, XIII, 153, n. 34.
[31] R. M. Grant, *Letter and the Spirit*.

advantageously in teaching their cosmogony. Each of the Homeric Olympian gods conveniently became an aspect or mode of the one universal fiery Spirit (or Logos). In this way the old titles could be used for the new "theology."

Similarly, later Judaism discovered a fourfold meaning in the Scriptures indicated by the word "paradise." There was (1) the simple or literal meaning, (2) the meaning arbitrarily imported into it (suggestion, *remez*), (3) the meaning deduced by investigation (*derush*), and (4) the theosophistic meaning (mystery, *sod*).[32] This mode of exegesis may have easily passed into the church with the "regulative norm of the Gospel," preserving her from the extravagances of the Jewish exegesis.

This regulative norm was especially necessary in her struggle with Gnosticism. The orthodox case against the Gnostic treatment of Scripture is trenchantly summarized by Tertullian:

> Now this heresy of yours does not receive certain Scriptures; and whichever of them it does receive, it perverts by means of additions and diminutions, for the accomplishment of its own purpose; and such as it does receive, it receives not in their entirety; but even when it does receive any up to a certain point as entire, it nevertheless perverts even these by the contrivance of diverse interpretations.[33]

Marcionites in particular were guilty of accepting only part of the Scriptures; Gnostics erred in the other two points. They both added to the orthodox canon and "perverted" it by their strange exegesis. One example of Gnostic interpretation of an accepted portion of the written Word will illustrate the difficulty the church faced.

When the Valentinians, one of the many sects of the Gnostics, wished to give proof of their doctrine of the *pleroma* (the Fulness, meaning a series of eternal beings or emanations from the supreme being) they turned to the prologue of the Gospel of John (*A.H.* I,8,5). According to Irenaeus, they interpreted the first verse to mean that the Word (Logos) was

---

[32] Schürer, *op. cit.*, II, 1, 348-349.
[33] *Presc.* 17. See also *A. H.* 1, 8-9. Irenaeus (*A. H.* III, 11, 7) lists four heresies, each of which uses one of the Gospels: Ebionites, Matthew; Marcionites, Luke; Adoptionists, Mark; and Valentinians, John.

located in the Beginning, or in the First Principle, and that the First Principle was in God. The Word then produced its partner, Life (John 1:4). These two in turn brought forth Man and Church (John 1:4). This group of four (Word, Life, Man, and Church) make up the second Tetrad (group of four) among the aeons. Where do we find the first Tetrad? That was revealed after the coming of the Savior. John 1:14 calls him "Only-begotten of the Father, full of Grace and Truth." These four, Only-Begotten, Father, Grace, and Truth, are the first Tetrad. In this way the Valentinians enlisted scriptural support for their aeons, tetrads, and ogdoads (group of eight). How could the orthodox meet this irrefutable authority of the written Word?

In her case against Marcion the church retained the Old Testament by interpreting it christologically, that is, she relied upon a view of the Old Covenant that saw Christ prophesied throughout. The Law and the Prophets had spoken not so much to their own contemporaries as to later generations. In this the church was only following the example of Christ Himself (Luke 24:44-47) and the apostles (I Cor. 10:1-4).

In the clash with the Gnostic sects, however, the orthodox found allegory a two-edged sword. It was turned back upon her with a vengeance, as the exegesis of the Valentinians so well illustrates. What answer could she give to a practice that she herself had used to such advantage against Marcionism?

Orthodox spokesmen neither denied the inspiration of Scripture nor rejected the allegorical method. They insisted instead that the starting point and the end of exegesis must be Christ. Against the Gnostic claim to a secret tradition they did not repudiate the use of tradition entirely but held that tradition must be open, genuine apostolic tradition. Thus in the end it was Christianity's roots in history that prevented her from drifting into the ethereal world of Gnostic philosophy. Just as Marcion tried to cut the church off from its roots in Old Testament history, so Valentinus tried to cut it off from the world. Irenaeus and Tertullian, however, insist on a theology anchored in history.

Irenaeus and Interpretation

Irenaeus complained that far from employing the Bible the heretics drew their doctrines from foreign sources (*A.H.* II,14,1-2) and then came to the Scriptures in order to support their system (*A.H.* I,8,1). In doing this they dismembered the order and meaning of the Scriptures. The absurd conclusions of this type of approach is shown by the heretics' denial that John's prologue speaks of the Lord Jesus Christ at all (*A.H.* I,9,2).

Convinced that this type of approach to the Scriptures is wrong, Irenaeus advocates an approach accompanied by a sound mind, devoted to piety, and with a love of truth (*A.H.* II,27,1; III,11,7). If this is done the Scriptures will not be mutilated but be found to be one harmonious whole, since the author and message are the same throughout (*A.H.* III, 12,11; IV,9,2). Moreover, if this proper approach is taken — coming only to seek the truth — the message of the writings will be easily understood, for the things that God intended for man are those that are easily observed and are clearly and unambiguously expressed in the Bible. The Scriptures will yield a like interpretation for everyone and the body of truth will remain complete without collision of its parts. Thus for Irenaeus the message of the Bible is unified, "all Scripture . . . perfectly consistent" (*A.H.* II,28,3).

But to speak of the clear sense of the Scriptures is not to deny certain obscurities. These, however, should not surprise us since we are so far inferior to the Author, the Word of God, and since even the physical world holds mysteries beyond our comprehension (*A.H.* II,28,2). While we must leave some mysteries to God, there are ways of handling difficult passages, a way of interpreting Scripture which Irenaeus calls "the method of discovery" (*A.H.* II,27,2). Difficult passages, like parables, numbers and enigmas, should be interpreted in the light of clear passages. It is not safe to build doctrine upon the obscure and insecure, as the Gnostic does, anymore than it is safe to build a house upon shifting sand (*A.H.* II,27,2-3). System (*regula*) does not spring from numbers but numbers from a system (*A.H.* II,25,1). Therefore problem passages must fit the clear ones or be left unanswered. Thus while Irenaeus was not himself free from the use of allegory, he did not, as the Gnostic, reach conclusions from the Scriptures at variance with the rule of faith.

A place remained in Irenaeus' thought for men of superior ability to bring out the meaning of the Bible, but these are not permitted to change the subject matter of the faith (*A.H.* I,10,3). As we noted when discussing the rule, Irenaeus used the body of Christian truth as a norm for the interpretation of Scripture (*A.H.* I,9,4), a norm, however, which coincided exactly with the results of correct biblical exegesis (*A.H.* II,27,2). This truth is that proclaimed by the church (*A.H.* I,9,4). Because of the Bishop's appeal to succession in this regard, some Roman Catholic authors feel that he is condemning private interpretation in favor of that delivered by the church.[34] This position, however, fails to explain certain clear statements in *Against Heresies* (*A.H.* II,27,1). What Irenaeus is saying is that an interpretation of the Scripture must not conflict with the truth, the faith, or the rule as it is possessed in the church. This is far different from saying that the individual must refrain from any interpretation until the rule is announced by the church.

Tertullian and Interpretation

The opponents of Tertullian, being the same as those of Irenaeus, are charged with the same wicked handling of the Scriptures, that is, of choosing parts of it or twisting the meaning of that portion chosen (*Presc.* 38). Tertullian's answer to their devices is much the same as Irenaeus'. While the New Testament advances beyond the Old Testament, it is not opposed to it (*Ag. Marc.* IV,11 and V,11). Tertullian uses in this connection the metaphor of the fruit separating from the seed. The obscure prophetic witness to the truth (*Apol.* 21,18) has been made manifest by Christ (*Ag. Prax.* 31).

For Tertullian, as for Irenaeus, the Bible is a whole and its parts are not contradictory. We should come to the Bible expecting to find its meaning from the sense of the words themselves but consistently with the guiding principle of all interpretation, the *disciplina rationis* (*Presc.* 9). Opinion

---

[34] A. Coan, *The Rule of Faith in Ecclesiastical Writings*, p. 81.

differs as to just what is intended by *disciplina rationis*, but the context seems to demand "the purport of Scripture." Tertullian mentions two matters: (1) the sense of the words, and (2) the *disciplina rationis*. Then he goes on to speak of the *words* and their *connections*. If in our Bible study we encounter difficult passages, such as parables or other figurative language, we must not do as the heretics and base our doctrine upon them (*Presc.* 17), but explain these in accordance with the rest (*Ag. Prax.* 26). If there is an apparent discrepancy in one or two passages, these must give way to the many (*On Modesty* 17).

As we have seen, in order to show that the heretic has no right to the Scriptures, Tertullian uses in his *Prescription Against Heretics* the argument based on "apostolic churches." Wherever one finds the true rule of faith there likewise will one find the true exposition of the Scriptures. The question is, What relation does one bear to the other? The North African apologist uses *regula* three times in connection with the interpretation of Scripture. In the *Prescription* 12, he says that the *regula* sets the limits of inquiry into the Scriptures. Only those speculations and questions that do not offend this norm are acceptable to true Christians. In *On Modesty* 8, he tells us that the heretic will not subject himself to the rule, but by using parables he makes the Bible say anything he pleases. In *Against Praxeas* 20, the Monarchians are accused of disregarding the rule and building their theories on a few passages. The rule of faith, then, is the doctrinal summation of the *whole* Bible (*Presc.* 38). There are not two guiding principles in interpreting the Scriptures: (1) the *regula,* and (2) the purport of Scripture; only one, because the two are essentially the same.

Summary

We conclude then that Irenaeus and Tertullian, as church spokesmen, countered the Gnostic appeal to an esoteric tradition as the key to the exegesis of the Bible with the following: (1) They asserted the historical basis of the gospel. (2) The apostles committed to the churches that they founded the truth they had received from Jesus Christ. (3) Christian truth is found in the apostolic writings and in the apostolic message preached in the churches. (4) There is no secret tradition necessary for a proper understanding of the Scriptures. (5) The Scriptures teach what the apostolic churches teach. The rule of faith and the results of proper interpretation of the Bible are the same. Together they set forth the truth of God brought by Jesus Christ.

VII

THE EARLY THIRD CENTURY: CLEMENT AND ORIGEN

G NOSTIC TEACHING, AFTER CREATING THE CRISIS TO WHICH Irenaeus and Tertullian speak, found a friendlier atmosphere in Egypt. Alexandria had been the home of two leading Gnostics, Valentinus and Basilides, and the disposition toward speculation, even among the orthodox of the East, was less inclined to slam the door in the face of Gnostic teaching.

Certain similarities to the Gnostic approach can be noted in the famous Catechetical School at Alexandria, where teachers were eager to press culture into the service of the church. The earliest known representative of orthodox Christianity in the city and perhaps the first head of the school was Pantaenus. According to Eusebius (*E.H.* V,10), Pantaenus preached among the people of the East and traveled as far as India, but his greatest contribution to the church seems to have been his teaching. One of his pupils says that he "engendered in the souls of his hearers a deathless element of knowledge." That pupil, Clement of Alexandria, was to become the real founder of Alexandrian theology.

Titus Flavius Clemens was born of pagan parents about

150. Showing early signs of scholarship, his search for truth sent him traveling for a time until he found his thirst satisfied by the teachings of Pantaenus. He was ordained a presbyter at Alexandria and from about 190 he instructed students in the Christian faith. When persecution of believers broke out in A.D. 202, Clement fled Alexandria and spent his later years probably in Cappadocia.

His influence, however, continued after his death through his writings. Among his works the three most important are the *Exhortation to the Greeks (Protreptikos)*, *The Instructor (Paidagōgos)*, and the *Miscellanies (Stromateis,* literally the "Carpet Bags"). In a passage at the beginning of *The Instructor* Clement explains the triple method by which the Logos gains our salvation. He first "converts" us *(protrepōn)*, then he "disciplines" us *(paidagōgōn)*, and finally he "instructs" us. Some students see in this passage a blueprint of the three works we have listed. While it is likely that Clement embodied his teaching in such a trilogy, it is not at all certain that the *Miscellanies* is the third of the three works.

Clement's ability has often been obscured by the extraordinary gifts of his successor, Origen, who is the most outstanding theologian of the pre-Nicene era. Origen was born about 185, probably at Alexandria, of Christian parents. During the persecution that drove Clement from the city, his father Leonides was martyred. When peace was restored the Bishop of Alexandria put Origen in charge of the instruction given to the catechumens. He gave himself to the task without reservation. He studied, he fasted, he prayed, he traveled. One trip took him to Rome, another to Arabia, and ill another to Antioch. When he visited Palestine in 23 he was ordained a presbyter. This action provoked har eelings in Alexandria, and upon his return to the city he was deprived of his position in the Church. Origen then left Egypt and settled at Caesarea in Palestine, teaching and preaching for the rest of his days. During the Decian persecution (249-250) he was imprisoned and tortured in an attempt to gain his recantation. He remained faithful but his health was broken. He died a short time later at Tyre.

Even his surviving works are too numerous to mention

here. They range over the fields of apologetics, exegesis, theology, and practical Christian experience. His most significant theological treatise is *On First Principles,* the most ambitious work of pre-Nicene times. From the viewpoint of a modern student the chief weakness showing through his writings is his lack of historical sense. This deeply affected his interpretation of the Bible and cut him loose from the conservativism of men like Irenaeus. Yet the disposition toward speculation in the Alexandrians opened up areas of study completely ignored by the men we have thus far examined.

For this and other reasons the Alexandrians deserve a place in our study. Not only do they give us a broader geographical foundation upon which to base our judgments, but their approach to the deposit of faith is unlike any we have yet encountered. Two characteristics above all others must be understood from the start. Gnosticism, as we have met it thus far, has been of the extreme (heretical) variety. Clement and Origen use the word "gnostic" in another sense, one very much like that employed in the *Epistle of Barnabas.* The Alexandrians mean by "gnostic" the Christian intellectual. His speculations have not actually carried him beyond orthodoxy, but his supposed gift of interpreting the Bible enables him to "know" the deep things of God. In that he is the custodian of hidden truth, the Alexandrians' gnostic replaces Irenaeus' bishop as the guardian of the faith.

A second characteristic of the Alexandrian approach relates specifically to authority. The norms of doctrinal truth in Egypt had not attained the fixity that we noted in the West. While Clement and Origen are aware of threatening heresy they are not as disturbed by it as their Western colleagues. Whatever their reasons for this, their canon of Scripture is more fluid; their tradition is not as closely linked to the institutional church; and their rule is not as precisely worded.

I. THE CREED

The Alexandrians contribute little to the information that we have already garnered on the creed. After Origen settled at Caesarea in the third decade of the third century he hints at some creed, very likely the one from his native Alexandria. In his *Commentary on John* (XXXII, 16) he points out that certain articles of faith are absolutely essential for salvation. Then he describes some of these.

> First of all believe that there is one God . . . We must also believe that Jesus Christ is Lord . . . And we must believe in the Holy Spirit, and that having free-will we are punished for our misdeeds and rewarded for our good deeds.

According to Origen, these articles form a unit of truth. Therefore, one cannot pick and choose at will. To take one example, one cannot reject the birth of Christ from the Virgin Mary and the Holy Spirit and accept his crucifixion under Pontius Pilate. The articles hang together.

Similar summaries of the faith occur elsewhere in Origen's writings. Their structure, like that of the above quotation, is based upon some triadic formula. Since the articles are also said to be necessary for salvation it seems best to regard them as some confession employed at baptism. Thus the only evidence of a creed that the Alexandrians contribute confirms the conclusion we have previously reached: 1) The earliest confessions were used in the service of baptism. 2) These were built on a triadic formula. 3) Declaratory creeds, as we know them today, emerged only in the second half of the third century.

II. TRADITION

Though the Alexandrians were unquestionably oriented to Christianity, they did breathe deeply of Greek philosophy, which, as we have seen, was not primarily a literary discipline. It was interested in the spoken word and the personal contact between teacher and pupil. This mood is reflected in Clement's view of tradition. He says, for instance, that Jesus did not "disclose to the many what did not belong to the many . . . secret things are entrusted to speech, not to writing, as is the case with God."[1]

Two concepts of tradition can be traced in Clement. One of them is public and ecclesiastical; the other esoteric and

---

[1] *Misc.* I. For a thorough discussion of Clement's view of secret tradition see R. P. C. Hanson, *Origen's Doctrine of Tradition*, ch. IV.

gnostic. The first of these is much like the rule of truth in Irenaeus and the rule of faith in Tertullian. Thus in certain passages Clement is quite conservative in his view of tradition.

But his leanings toward Christian gnosticism with its concept of a higher spirituality resulted in other statements about a secret tradition like the one above. In these statements it is not always clear just what Clement does intend by tradition. Its function is not clearly distinguished from its content. Hanson concludes that Clement has confused three separate things in his theory of secret tradition: 1) his own private speculations, 2) a tradition of doctrinal speculations inherited from eminent teachers before him, and 3) the church's interpretation of her tradition in teaching and preaching.[2] What remains clear is Clement's essential orthodoxy. His so-called secret tradition does not supersede either the public tradition of the church or the Scriptures.

Fortunately the meaning of tradition in Origen's writings is much clearer. Like Clement he also knows of an ecclesiastic tradition (*Com. Ser. on Matt.* 46) and a secret tradition. In contrast to Clement, however, he gives no direct and continuous ancestry for his secret tradition apart from the Bible. Nor does he confuse secret tradition with the public rule of faith. He keeps the two quite distinct. His secret tradition is derived from the Bible by the intellectual elite of the church. It consists of a number of esoteric doctrines that are beyond the understanding of the average believer. Origen assumes that Christ and his apostles taught these doctrines privately to their more intelligent followers, just as Origen teaches his.

There is no evidence, however, that Origen believed in the existence of any continuity between this alleged secret tradition of Jesus' apostles and his own secret doctrines.[3] When he speaks of secret tradition he simply intends doctrines derived from the Bible that are accessible to everyone, but that overtax the spiritual and intellectual powers of the average Christian. The pressing question is, How does this secret tradition relate to the rule?

[2] Hanson, *ibid.*, pp. 71-72.
[3] *Ibid.*, p. 87.

III. THE RULE OF FAITH

In the writings of Irenaeus and Tertullian the rule of faith combines two ideas, the faith of the church and the interpretation of the Bible. The same is true in the works of the Alexandrians. The first of these ideas is prominent in Clement's phrases "the rule of the church" and "the ecclesiastical rule" (*Misc.* VI,15; VII,7; I,19). It is not always clear, however, that Clement means by this rule, as Irenaeus and Tertullian meant, the truth held by all the faithful. He urges loyalty to the rule of the church but on several occasions he clearly has in mind the Christian gnostic's standard of faith in contrast to the ordinary believer (*Misc.* IV,16; V,1 and VII,3).

When the rule is related to the Bible it is equated with the church's interpretation of Scripture (*Misc.* VII,16). Clement urges his readers to hand on the proper exegesis of the Bible according to the rule of truth (*Misc.* VI,15). In fact, those who best understand the Scriptures are those who receive and observe them according to the ecclesiastical rule. The rule then may also be thought of as "the concord and harmony of the Law and the Prophets in the covenant handed down at the coming of the Lord" (*Misc.* VI,15).

In view of all of his statements, Clement's idea of the church's rule must start out with the simple beliefs of all believers, beliefs derived from the Bible, and then pass beyond these into the secret tradition of the gnostic. Since he declares that both the *gnōsis* and the *kanōn* are a harmony of the Scriptures, it is impossible to maintain that he preserved any clear distinction between secret tradition and the church's rule of faith.[4] To deny this would force us to suppose that he conceived of two separate traditions, each consisting of a harmony of the Scriptures.

Interestingly and in contrast to Irenaeus, Clement thought of this rule as the tradition preserved in the church, not by a succession of bishops, but by a series of teachers who had originally received it from the Lord's apostles (*Misc.* I,1). Such a tradition was not accessible to the average believer. It was given only to the few whom the Lord knew it con-

---

[4] *Ibid.*, p. 61.

cerned. In this view Clement combines the orthodox idea of an apostolic tradition with the Gnostic idea of eminent teachers who possess special intellectual powers. Such an idea was not uncommon in the Alexandrian atmosphere. Both Philo and the *Epistle of Barnabas* use a similar theme.

This affinity to his predecessors at Alexandria, especially in the use of allegory, helps to account for Clement's obscurity concerning the function of his *kanōn* and its content (*Misc.* VI,15). It is certain that his rule includes a number of speculations that find no direct support in the apostolic writings or, as far as we are able to determine, in any oral tradition. But it is best to hold with Prestige that Clement meant by the *kanōn* no source of information complementary to Holy Writ but an explanatory key that the Savior delivered to the apostles.[5] Clement's *gnōsis* then, like Barnabas' before him, turns out to be the allegorical understanding of the Scriptures.

Origen agrees with his predecessor in his view of the rule, but in some important respects differs from him. His most common term for the rule is *kanōn*, but *kerygma* and others are also used. Like those before him, Origen relates the rule very closely to the teaching of the church. In his *Sermon on Jeremiah* V, 14 he identifies the *kanōn* with "the church's principles" and the "intention of sound teaching," while in his *Commentary on Matthew* he says to disbelieve that the words of the Scriptures represent what Jesus really said would be going contrary to "the church's principles" (XVII,35). Unlike Clement, Origen will speak at times of this rule of faith prevalent among the majority of the church in contrast to the beliefs of the Christian intellectual (*Comm. on John* XIII,16).

Other of Origen's references to the rule identify it very closely with the Bible. For example, in his *On First Principles* he says that it is necessary to conform the mind to the rule and "to think of the Holy Spirit's words not as a composition depending upon feeble human eloquence" (IV,3,14). Can we therefore identify the rule with the Spirit-inspired

---

[5] G. L. Prestige, *Fathers and Heretics*, pp. 17-18.

Scriptures? Or did Origen conceive of the rule as a source of doctrine independent of the Bible? While it would not be entirely accurate to say that the Bible is the rule of faith, Origen never thought of Christian truth coming from any other source. Despite the many speculations found in his writings, the great Alexandrian always felt that these were the natural outgrowth of sound biblical exegesis. But, in contrast to his attitude toward the Bible, Origen did not hesitate to set aside the rule of faith if he felt that he could improve upon it. Had he felt that the rule was an independent source of doctrine, he would never have consciously superseded it even as he did not the Bible.

Origen's rule is best described then as the Christian faith as it was preached and taught by the churches of his day and as it had been preached and taught since the days of the apostles. While he could speak of it as consisting of articles, he nowhere identifies it with a creed, nor, for that matter, with the Scriptures. Its content, however, was the same as the Bible's and it was demonstrated from the Bible.[6] It was simply the Christian interpretation of the Bible taught in the churches.

In the end, then, Origen's rule does not differ greatly from the rule of Irenaeus and Tertullian. He is not as ready to apply it as an exegetical norm and he would not be able to express it as clearly as Tertullian, but like them he considers it the sum of biblical teaching. Clement is less "orthodox." He stresses the train of teachers within the church and identifies the rule with the esoteric teaching of this intellectual elite, something Origen never does, but then Clement's rule is as much a hermeneutic as it is a body of doctrine. And even Clement's gnostic had to submit to the authority of the Bible.

IV. THE SCRIPTURES

While differences between them appear elsewhere, Clement and Origen agree in their views of the Bible. It is for them *the* source of Christian doctrine. For instance, in *Miscellanies* VII, 16, Clement indicates that even the Christian gnostic

---
[6] Hanson, *op. cit.*, p. 113.

must bow to the Scriptures as interpreted by the church. This was his basic attitude. Unfortunately he did not always maintain it.[7]

Similarly Origen, whose speculations have a way of drifting far from the faith at times, always claims to find his doctrines in the Scriptures. "He takes very little notice of credal forms and never implies that they have any authority independent of that of the Bible."[8] Most important of all he, unlike Clement, never quotes any other authoritative source than the Scriptures for his teachings. For example, he finds no way of explaining and bringing to man's knowledge the teaching about the Son of God except by means of the Gospels and the writings of the apostles (*First Prin.* I,3,1). He assumes that the deciding factor in any discussion is always Holy Writ. This remained his constant attitude.

The Canon

By the Bible the Alexandrians mean both the Old and the New Testaments. Their testimony indicates that the place achieved by the apostolic writings was not limited to the West. We have seen that the church had become accustomed to thinking of at least twenty of the twenty-seven books that make up our New Testament as canonical. The Alexandrians also accept these. Their witness, therefore, is most important concerning the fate of the other seven books: James, II Peter, II and III John, Jude, Hebrews, and Revelation.[9]

Clement gives clear testimony to II John, Jude, Hebrews, and Revelation. Perhaps he omits III John because he did not know of it, although he might have thought it scarcely worth mentioning because of its shortness and similarity to some expressions in II John. Whatever his reasons, he ignores it as he does James and II Peter.

Because of his travels Origen must be considered an unusually important witness for the history of the New Testament canon. Everywhere he visited — Rome, Syria, Athens, Cappadocia, and Arabia — he acquired a knowledge of what books were canonical. Consequently, he divides the "books

---

[7] *Ibid.*, p. 49.
[8] *Ibid.*, p. 126.
[9] C. R. Gregory, *The Canon and Text of the New Testament*, p. 222.

of the church" into those "recognized everywhere" and those disputed in certain churches. Among those received everywhere are the four Gospels, Paul's letters, Acts, I Peter, I John, and Revelation — practically the same list as Irenaeus gave to us a half century earlier. The disputed books, according to Origen, are Hebrews, II Peter, II and III John, James, Jude, the *Letter of Barnabas,* the *Shepherd of Hermas,* and the *Didache.* All of these Origen himself accepts, with the possible exceptions of II and III John. He expresses doubt as to their genuineness.[10]

The combined testimony of Clement and Origen supports the authoritative status of the New Testament books, but it shows the lack of any "official list." Origen's test of authority seems to be the use of a book in the churches of his day. There is no reference to any authority more official than this. The prior question, Why did the churches use these particular books? must find its answer in the books' authorship and in the tradition they possessed in the churches, though even these were not decisive. Much also depended upon the books' inherent quality, in other words, their inspiration. The great exegete says of Hebrews: "If I were to give my opinion, I would say that the thoughts are those of the apostle, but the style and the composition belong to one who is relating from memory the apostolic teaching. . . ."[11] It was the content that made the vital difference.

Inspiration

Origen, like Irenaeus and Tertullian before him, believed in the inspiration of the Scriptures. He lists the composition of the Scriptures by the Spirit of God among those doctrines handed down to all believers by the apostles (*First Prin.* I, pref., 8 and I,3,1). And the importance of the doctrine to Origen personally is shown by his willingness to devote one of the four books of his *On First Principles* — the fourth and last one — to this theme. This book opens with an *apologia* for the divine character of the Scriptures. The wide acceptance of Christianity and the fulfillment of Jesus' words,

---

[10] A. Souter, *Text and Canon of the New Testament,* pp. 182-183.
[11] Eusebius, *E. H.,* VI, 25, 13.

Origen asserts, prove that the Scriptures are divine (*First Prin.* IV,1,2). But if anyone insists on more evidence, let him consider the daring venture and success of the apostles. These should indicate that their command was from God (*First Prin.* IV, 1,5). Anyone who is willing to approach the prophetic writings with care and attention will feel from his reading that they are of divine inspiration, and not the compositions of men (*First Prin.* IV,1,6). Yet even if men do not recognize the divine influence that extends through all the prophetic writings, that does not alter their true character (*First Prin.* IV,1,7).

The New Testament, Origen feels, is a necessary counterpart to the Old. The same Holy Spirit was in the prophets and the apostles (*First Prin.* II,7,1 and IV,1,15); but the Old Testament was not self-authenticating, "for before the advent of Christ it was not possible to bring forward clear proofs of the divine inspiration of the old Scriptures" (*First Prin.* IV,1,6). Not that they were not inspired prior to the incarnation; indeed they were, but only after Christ's coming did their inspiration become known. In other words, Christ's appearing added an *apologia* for the inspiration of the Old Testament.

Interpretation

It is a well-known fact that Alexandrian exegesis, based upon this view of inspiration, was allegorical. Regardless of other differences, the successive writers — Philo, Barnabas, Clement, and Origen — are alike in this respect. Clement had a definite theory of the threefold sense of the Scriptures (*Misc.* I,28 and VI,15). But Origen was to give the theory its most elaborate treatment.

Origen complains that the reason for impious and ignorant assertions about God is that men, interpreting the Bible according to the bare letter, fail to understand its spiritual sense. This is why the Jew fails to see Christ in the prophecies and why the Gnostic, taking some passages literally (Deuteronomy 32:22; Amos 3:6; etc.), thinks that the Creator is not perfect or good and that the Savior came to proclaim another God (*First Prin.* IV,1,8). Interestingly Tertullian and Irenaeus charged the Gnostic with interpreting the Scriptures too freely. Now Origen criticizes his literalism.

In giving his own method of interpreting the written Word, Origen was not conscious of any novelty. He was simply summarizing that method which appears right to anyone who keeps the rule of the church (*First Prin.* IV,1,9), since this method is drawn from the Scriptures themselves (*First Prin.* IV,1,11).

The Scriptures, according to Origen, possess a threefold meaning comparable to the nature of man: body, soul, and spirit. For the simple-minded the obvious interpretation, the flesh of the Scriptures, was there. For the man who has made some spiritual progress there is that meaning which edifies the soul. But for the "perfect" man there is a spiritual meaning. The bodily part of the Scriptures, not entirely unprofitable, is capable of improving the man who receives it. But the Spirit intended to set forth spiritual events and truths. In order to do this it was necessary at times, though not often, to record events that did not actually happen. These should not be confused with the spiritual truth being presented (*First Prin.* IV,1,15), truth dealing primarily with God, the coming of the Son, his nature, his mission, with the other rational creatures, evil, the nature of the world, and the cause of its existence (*First Prin.* IV,1,14). Some of these themes led Origen some distance from accepted ecclesiastical teaching, but he felt all of them to be the true teaching of the Bible spiritually understood.

Summary

What may we say now by way of summary? For all of the writers of the late second and early third centuries the rule and the Scriptures interact upon each other to provide the fundamental expression and source of Christian doctrine. For Irenaeus the rule is expressed in the Scriptures, but it may also be ascertained by heeding the teaching of the Church through her proper bishops and presbyters. It serves as a series of boundary markers for biblical exegesis. For Tertullian the rule is the theological system expressed in the message of the apostles. Whether written (the Bible) or oral (the teaching of the apostolic churches) it is in reality one and the same. This rule, just as for Irenaeus, provides the limits beyond which doctrinal inquiry and Scriptural interpretation must not go. In the thought of Clement of Alexandria unwritten tradition has an unusual place. The rule, preserved by a series of teachers who derived it ultimately from the apostles, contains teaching not accessible to the average believer and probably not derived from the apostolic writings, though it is difficult to distinguish its function (a method of interpretation) from its content. Origen, in contrast to Clement, consistently resorts to the Bible for his teaching (at least this was his intention). The rule for him, though the same in content, was inferior to the Bible in authority, for unlike the Bible it could be improved.

VIII

THE SUM OF IT

JESUS CHRIST IS THE SUPREME AUTHORITY FOR ALL CHRIStians. There has never been any doubt about this fact in the historic church. As the incarnate Son he taught as one having authority (Mark 1:22). He cast out unclean spirits (Mark 1:27); he forgave sins (Mark 2:10); he modified the provisions of the Law (Matt. 5:21,27,33); and he claimed that he would be man's final judge (John 5:27) — all on the basis of his own divine authority. Standing at history's mid-point, the period of the incarnation, and at history's end, the second advent, he sums up in himself God's purposes for humanity.

During this age, the period between the incarnation and the parousia, God grants to relative authorities a claim upon man's obedience. In the civil realm he has given power to earthly rulers (Romans 13:1-2). In the functioning of the church he distributes a measure of authority to leaders (II Cor. 10:13). And for the teaching of the church he has called and endowed select men called apostles (Acts 1:8; 21-22).

Christian theology during this time faces a double task. It must "hold fast the form of sound words" (II Tim. 1:13) and it must witness of Christ "unto the uttermost part of the earth" (Acts 1:8). By preserving and propagating the first-century message, it fulfills an apostolic ministry. By going into all the world in every age, it carries out a catholic mission. If it is to be true it must preach the Word; if it is to be relevant it must speak to the times. Christian theology is thus a blending of the changeless with the changing.

The classical "protestant" approach to authority, while not ignoring the development of doctrine, tries to anchor theology in the changeless by emphasizing the apostolic witness of Scripture. The "catholic" approach to authority, while professing to be truly apostolic, underscores the *magisterium*, the living authority of the church. Hence the problem of Scripture and tradition. A brief statement of these two positions will afford us a perspective for the summation of second-century views of doctrinal authority.

The "protestant" position, classically expressed, for example, in the Westminster Confession of Faith, asserts that Scripture is the rule of faith and practice for Christians. The authority of Scripture, which calls for faith and obedience, depends neither upon the testimony of men nor upon that of the church. God, who alone is Truth, is its author and its witness. He, by a work of the Holy Spirit in our minds and hearts, persuades us of the divine authority of the Bible.

Though the Scriptures speak with this authority, they do not eliminate the need for ordering some circumstances of church life, such as matters of worship and church government, according to the light of "nature" and Christian prudence. In a word, there is a legitimate place for ecclesiastical tradition. Only let the church constantly bring its practices and customs to the test of Scripture so that if any prove contrary to Holy Writ they may be abandoned.

Nor does the authority of Scripture eliminate the ministry of gifted teachers of the Word. All things in Scripture are not alike plain in themselves, nor clear to all. Only those things necessary for salvation are clearly presented. Therefore God has given to some men within the church the gift of teaching the truth of God. By explaining difficult passages in the light of clear ones, these teachers meaningfully

The Sum of It 141

minister the Word. But their infallible rule of interpretation of Scripture remains Scripture itself.

The Word, so interpreted, is that canon bequeathed to the church of all ages by the Lord and his apostles. The determination of which books carry divine authority was a long process, but the important thing to understand is that when a decision was rendered it came, not from councils or Popes, but from the faithful everywhere submitting to the apostolic character of the writing. The books were not so much the product as the basis of the churches' decision.

The "catholic" position represented by *The Catholic Encyclopedia* article on "Tradition and the Living Magisterium" asks the Protestant, "By what right do you rest on Sunday, not Saturday? How can you consider infant baptism as valid? In short, do you not have certain practices which are not strictly Biblical? There must be a place given to tradition." The catholic believes that the Bible is the Church's book. Its canonicity and its interpretation must be by the Church. The Bible simply does not carry with it the guarantee of its divinity, its authenticity, or its meaning. These must come from some other source, the Church. Therefore, the believer must make an act of faith in the intermediary authority between the Word of God and his reading.

But that, argues the "catholic," is as it ought to be. God never intended Scripture to be the sole authority for faith and practice. He gave to his Church certain other revealed truths that complete those from the Bible. The Council of Trent (1545-1563) called these truths "unwritten traditions from the apostles." But in more recent days, since the Vatican Council of 1870, the Roman Catholic looks upon tradition less in terms of unwritten apostolic teaching and more in terms of revealed truth living in "the mind of the Church," or preferably, in "the present thought of the Church in continuity with her traditional thought." From the many obscure and confused formulas out of the past the teaching office of the Church, called the *magisterium,* adopts the true and rejects the false. Thus tradition has a double meaning for the catholic. It is both the divine truth coming down to the present generation in the "mind of the church" and its guardianship by the organ of the living *magisterium,* which is for Roman Catholics the episcopate headed by the Pope.

Both unwritten tradition and the Bible come under this guardianship. The Church through the *magisterium* determines the canon, specifies the rules for interpreting the Bible, and even restricts the use of the Bible and its publication if it considers "the endless discussion" and "the abuses of every kind" a danger to the faithful. Thus the final authority in the Catholic position is the living voice of the Church. It not only presents the truth, it also imposes it upon the faithful.

The Roman Catholic doctrine of tradition, which amounts to a theory not unlike continuous inspiration, permits the Church to develop and impose teachings that have no basis in Scripture. When the bodily assumption of Mary was promulgated in 1950 it was imposed upon the faithful as a binding dogma even though it was devoid of any biblical support. Clearly from this instance it is not necessary for the Roman Catholic Church to base its dogmas on Scripture. It is enough that Mary is full of grace and free from the curse of sin. The dogma, it is argued, is part of the total theology of Mary and intimately linked with the idea that Christ and Mary are inseparable. This is sufficient.

Thus the Bible can be ignored or overridden in the name of the living *magisterium*. Is this not proof of the statement "whenever another source of knowledge is placed alongside Scripture as being of equal value, Scripture is eventually relegated to the background?"

The sharp difference between the "protestant" and the "catholic" approach to the norms of doctrine is clear. To one the Church is under the Word; to the other, the Word is under the Church. We must now ask, To what degree does the second-century witness support or refute either position?

An extended glance will reveal that the second century is not a "protestant" period as some evangelicals understand that term. With a few important exceptions, evangelical Protestants (in contrast to liberal Protestants, who have surrendered the supernatural character of the Bible) are not characterized by the "churchmanship" that appears in the early centuries. In attempting to be contemporaries of our

THE SUM OF IT 143

Lord and his apostles, or "biblicists," they tend to minimize the importance of that community in which the Bible is authoritative. They take little or no account of the church in history. But the Bible is not the Koran or the Book of Mormon. It did not come down directly from heaven. Both the writing of the New Testament and the process of determining the canon took place within the living experience of the church, a fact "catholics" are quick to point out.

No one acquainted with the facts will deny that tradition was chronologically prior to the New Testament Scriptures, provided it is made clear that it is *apostolic* tradition that is prior. Tradition in the sense of "handing down" the truth of God was at first oral. Only later did it include the writings of the apostles alongside the proclamation of the *kerygma*. The convert's acceptance of the Christian message was expressed in a baptismal confession, which formed the nucleus of the faith. This too was practiced from the earliest days of the church. Thus the gospel message and the baptismal confession in the life of the church and in the experience of the individual Christian preceded the apostolic writings as a standard of truth.

In addition, the church had her ordered life and worship before her writings. The dictum that "it is the controversial which is discussed, the accepted which is assumed" applies especially to the silences of the New Testament concerning the sacraments and the ministry. Though we know very little about early liturgical (if we do not think of that term too narrowly) practices, it is enough to indicate that some simple liturgy preceded the apostolic writings. Such practices must have informally exerted an influence upon the minds of believers in matters of doctrine. Certainly the gospel was visible from the first in the baptism of believers and in their subsequent fellowship around the Lord's Supper.

But, perhaps most important of all, the acceptance of the books of the canon themselves took place within the worshiping and witnessing community. While it cannot be doubted that the test above all others for the canonicity of a book was its authorship or sponsorship by an apostle, it would be misleading to suppose that this was the only consideration. That Christian books were used in public worship by Justin's time is clearly stated by the Apologist (I *Apol.* 67) and, as we have seen, at least by Origen's day the use of a book by the churches supported its claim to canonical status even when its apostolic authorship was not accepted. The response of the churches, while not determinative, did count for something.

This combined evidence — oral preaching, liturgical practice, and tests of canonicity — indicates that the Bible was in some sense the church's book. This fact raises certain questions: Has evangelical Protestantism, particularly in its American expression, made enough room for history? Do we have an adequate doctrine of the church? Is there no legitimate place for tradition? We shall return to these questions after considering to what degree the second century was "catholic" in its view of authority.

The witness of the second century conflicts with the "catholic" position at four points: 1) tradition, 2) succession, 3) canonicity, and 4) exegesis. 1) If the uses of the word *paradosis* (*traditio*) suggest anything, it is that the early church did not think of tradition in terms of "the mind of the church." Its united witness is that the tradition, which is normative in the church, is apostolic. There is no suggestion that the rule of faith or the early confessions contained any doctrine not also found in the Scriptures. And the idea that tradition "completes" the Scripture is nowhere to be found.

Whatever influence the liturgical tradition may have exerted upon doctrine, such tradition had no authority for anything ruled out by Scripture.[1] Both Irenaeus and Tertullian, who is the first to use *traditio* in the sense of ecclesiastical traditions, make this clear. An ecclesiastical observance may be established provided it is agreeable to God (*The Chaplet* 4). If it lacks Scriptural warrant then good reason must be assigned for it, but if it is contrary to Scripture it must be abandoned (*On Fasting* 10). Clearly by Irenaeus' time apostolic tradition and Scripture were coterminous.

2) The "catholic" often cites the episcopal succession to which Irenaeus and Tertullian appeal as evidence for the Church's guardianship of the Bible. That a succession argu-

---

[1] Irenaeus' *Epistle to Florinus,* Eusebius, *E. H.,* V, 20, 6.

ment was used is not questioned. The argument was the only weapon readily available with which to meet the Gnostic claim to a secret and unwritten tradition. But the testimony is a two-edged sword. While it does indicate Irenaeus' and Tertullian's "churchmanship" and the prestige of the Church at Rome, it was primarily a means to an end, namely, to determine which message, Gnostic or orthodox, was apostolic. The argument does not imply, as A. C. Headlam long ago pointed out, any succession by ordination.[2] No doubt the bishops were ordained, but there is no idea that the validity of their ordination depended upon their place in the succession or that the succession depended upon any spiritual gifts received at ordination.

Only later was continuity of teaching, the second-century argument, replaced by the identity of the authority, the "catholic" argument, and by the theory that the Pope was the successor, not of the apostles, but of Peter.

Alexandria, representing another principle entirely, shows that the argument was far from universal. There succession meant a series of teachers in the church rather than a list of bishops. Apparently the succession argument served best as an antidote to the Gnostic peril in the West. But even there it had its limitations. It assumed the orthodoxy of the presbyters and had nothing to say about conflicts between "apostolic sees" themselves. Such deficiencies led in time to its abandonment in favor of synodal action.

In any case, the second-century argument, designed to determine which teaching was apostolic, was not thought of as a source of information that supplemented the Scriptures. Hegessipus, Irenaeus, and Tertullian nowhere suggest that teachers in the episcopal line delivered any truth other than that found in the canon. Orthodox "tradition" was either raw material that became Scripture or the explication of what was contained in Scripture. It was the Gnostic who used the "catholic" argument that the truth of Scripture cannot be understood by those ignorant of a secret tradition

[2] A. C. Headlam, *The Doctrine of the Church and Christian Reunion*, p. 126.

independent of Scripture and who thereby made unwritten tradition the ultimate authority for doctrine.

3) What we know of second-century tradition that was independent of Scripture, rather than affirming the presence of unwritten apostolic tradition, strongly supports the unique priority of written apostolic tradition. The apocryphal literature rejected by the early church shows that by the middle of the second century would-be authors of lives of Christ had no other trustworthy contact with the apostolic witness than through the Gospels and other New Testament works. Moreover, even within orthodox circles the "mind of the church" was sub-apostolic in some important respects. Recent investigation has shown, for instance, how the generation following the apostles failed to grasp the Pauline doctrine of grace. And yet the selection of the twenty-seven books that now comprise our New Testament give the greatest place to Paul. Thus the reception of the Pauline corpus as canonical set the doctrine of justification by faith forever before the church by lifting it out of the quagmire of the "mind of the church."

One is always inclined to ask the modern Roman Catholic view of authority why any canon was established at all. If the church is not under the Word, then why is a Word necessary except to add to those "formulas and monuments from the past" that provide the raw material for forming today's "mind of the church." What kind of "rule" is it that does not rule? What sort of standard is it that is not standard? As Oscar Cullmann argues, if the fixing of the canon had been carried out on the assumption that the Church's living *magisterium* should be set alongside or above the canon, then the reason for the creation of a canon becomes unintelligible.[3]

But can it be argued that the establishment of the canon itself was by the living *magisterium*? The Roman Catholic position regards canonicity as "the correlative of inspiration, being the extrinsic dignity belonging to writings which have been officially declared as of sacred origin and authority."[4] If by "officially declared" the Church of Rome means either

---

[3] O. Cullmann, "Tradition," *The Early Church*, p. 92.
[4] G. J. Reid, "Canon of the Holy Scriptures," *Catholic Encyclopedia* III, 267.

conciliar action or papal decree, then there is no historical evidence for such action in the second century, when at least twenty of the twenty-seven books of the New Testament were accepted as canonical. Whatever may have been the motives behind it, the approval of these books came from the scattered assemblies themselves, not from Popes or councils, whose voices are conspicuously silent.

Only two councils could possibly be claimed by Roman Catholics for this "official declaration." In 382 Pope Damascus summoned Jerome, the noted biblical scholar, to Rome to participate in a council of eclectic character. From this council came a list of books corresponding to our present New Testament. But this council was in no sense ecumenical and the principle of the canon had long before been established and the books been in use.

The other council is the Council of Trent, which gave in Session IV, 1546, the most explicit statement of the Roman Catholic canon to this day. The fact that the statement came after 1500 years of church history causes no particular problem for the Roman Catholic. John Henry Newman argues in his *The Development of Christian Doctrine* that "from the first age of Christianity its teaching looked toward those ecclesiastical dogmas, afterward recognized and defined." Often only after considerable time do such teachings become "so pronounced as to justify their definition."[5] Hence, whenever the definition of the canon came, its promulgation by the Church guarantees the papal guardianship from the beginning — evidence to the contrary notwithstanding.

4) This authority of the Church carries over to the interpretation of Scripture. The Pope must have been the authoritative interpreter of Holy Scripture in the second century because the Vatican Council in 1870 declared it so. But no such evidence is forthcoming from the witnesses that we have examined. Admittedly, Rome, according to Irenaeus and Tertullian, was the leading voice of the apostolic tradition, but these Fathers nowhere suggest that this prestige carried with it any gift of infallibility. On the contrary, in his case against the Gnostics, Irenaeus makes a special point of the

[5] Chap. IV, Introduction.

Bible's clarity concerning the major doctrines of the faith, the very point made by the Westminster Confession.

In the end the problem of the authority Scripture and tradition merges into the wider problem of the nature of the church. The Roman Catholic considers the Church the Body of Christ. His divine life is a continuing reality through the organs of continuity — the sacraments and the ministry. Dispensed through divine teaching and through sacramental grace, this life belongs to that divine order established in the incarnation of the Son of God. Each succeeding generation receives it through properly ordained bishops, successors of the apostles, and especially through the Pope, the successor of Peter. This hierarchical institution founded by Christ in Peter is infallibly guarded from error by a special grace exercised by the Pope when he speaks *ex cathedra* (officially) on matters of faith or morals. Under these conditions whatever the Church declares must be right because the only test of right is what the Church declares.

The evangelical Protestant views the church and its authority from the central and controlling authority of the gospel. He must believe everything in the degree to which it is essential to the new life created by that gospel. Thus the church, insofar as it is expressive of the good news of salvation and itself created by the power of it, shares in its authority. So it is with the ministry. It is an office, not an order. Being drawn from the gospel and created to serve the gospel, it is above all a ministry of the Word.

Is the evangelical committed to an unqualified biblicism? Is there no place for "tradition" in any sense? If in unwritten tradition the church is not addressed but is in conversation with itself, as Karl Barth puts it, is that conversation valueless?[6] Must the evangelical be a rebel against the communion of saints and 2000 years of spiritual history?

If our final authority is God, who reveals himself through the gospel, then we must recognize the authority of the church, created by and herald of the gospel. Salvation is into a family, a kingdom, a body, and a church. The soul truly humbled by the good news of salvation will not think of limiting God's truth to his own small experience. Further-

---

[6] *Church Dogmatics*, I, 1, 118.

more, complete rejection of tradition is an impossibility. Any biblicist who will carefully examine his own denomination will find certain characteristics that fail to rally explicit New Testament support. But isn't that what one would expect in any religious group that takes seriously history and human need?

G. L. Prestige makes a distinction between the early Christian use of tradition as *paradosis* and as *didaskalia*.[7] The former, as we have seen, was especially associated with apostolic truth. The latter denoted an accretion, enlargement, and confirmation of the faith. Any religious movement that operates within human affairs and is not concerned solely with individualistic mysticism will develop its own *didaskalia*. What of Sunday Schools, missionary societies, Easter, and instrumental music in worship services of our own day? Must these be jettisoned as "unbiblical"?

At the same time we cannot assume that every development or enlargement of the faith is a healthy one. If Christianity is true, it is because it has received an unchanging gospel. While the church ought to translate the biblical message into the language of the day, it must recognize that while doing so it is not binding future generations of believers to its testimony in the same way the apostles bound future ones to theirs. If the church is to have its proper sphere of authority it must not usurp the authority of Christ and his Word. "Our Savior is our authority," writes P. T. Forsythe. "Our mediatorial Christ leaves no room for a mediatorial Church."[8] The continuing life of the church is set under the authority of the Word of God, mediated by the unique ministry of the apostles.

But how does the evangelical Christian avoid replacing the personal Pope by a paper one? Is the finality of the Bible in any sense compatible with the Lordship of Christ? It is. The gospel through which the believer confronts Christ is uniquely expressed in the Bible. The appeal to divine truth in the Scriptures during the second century can be explained

---

[7] *Fathers and Heretics*, p. 5.
[8] *The Principle of Authority*, p. 372.

in no other way. Instead of obscuring Christ, as the church has often done, the Bible reveals him. This is because the writers were more than "eminent Christians." They were heralds of God's truth, unique instruments of God's self-disclosure. And the Spirit who revealed the truth to them bears witness to that truth in the hearts of the believer.

Thus Word, Spirit, and church find their proper place. The Scriptures, themselves a product of the Spirit's inspiring action upon chosen men, are the external channel of the internal witness of the Spirit in the believer. In this way the Bible is the voice of delegated authority within the Christian church for all ages. The church, as the community of believers and the home of the Spirit, possesses limited administrative authority. It cannot claim an unqualified power to command, but it does exercise provisional authority as hearer of God's Word. The Spirit is the teacher; the church is the taught; and the Word of God is that which is taught.

Only by the recognition of the proper place of each of these can evangelicalism counter the competitive claims to men's allegiance. Is the Gnostic crisis, created by the blending of a professed adherence to the Bible with the preaching of "another gospel," forever dead? No, in her *Science and Health* Mrs. Eddy claims, "As adherents of Truth, we take the inspired Word of the Bible as our sufficient guide to eternal life."[9] Is this not revived Gnosticism? What can simple biblicism say? Will not debate with the modern cults end in a draw, each side professing endlessly to give the true interpretation?

Second-century Christians would label modern cultic doctrines perversions of the gospel that created the church, of the truth professed in baptism, and of the rule of faith everywhere believed by the faithful. In a word, cultic doctrines fail to meet the test of apostolic tradition. But tradition in this sense is not to be looked upon as a continuous source of truth alongside the writings of the apostles. This tradition is Christianity itself, a legacy from the apostles, embedded in all the organs of the church's institutional life. It is, at the

---

[9] M. B. Eddy, *Science and Health*, p. 497.

same time, the purport of Scripture, and a guide for proper exegesis of its details. Where this message, the gospel, is preached and visibly presented in the sacraments (or ordinances), there is the church and all truth necessary for eternal salvation.

APPENDIX A

THE WORK OF THE HOLY SPIRIT

In order to counter the challenge of alien thought the early church turned to the canon of Scripture and to the rule of faith in those churches established by the apostles. The erection of these doctrinal standards consumed much of the church's theological energy. It is not surprising that the Holy Spirit's role in a full pattern of authority was given less than adequate attention. The witness to the work of the Spirit that we do find in the early Fathers is more than suggestive, but it is not integrated into a complete scheme of authority as we might desire.

The second-century witnesses speak of the Holy Spirit in three connections: 1) as the Voice of prophecy, 2) as the Inspirer of the Scriptures, and 3) as the Witness to divine truth within the heart of the believer.[1] What is important is that in no case did Christian writers regard the work of the Spirit as a substitute for those doctrinal norms that we have considered: the confession, the canon, the rule, and the tradition.

[1] The classic work on the Holy Spirit in the early church remains *The Holy Spirit in the Ancient Church* by H. B. Swete. This appendix is largely a digest of Swete's work concentrating upon the Spirit as a factor in the pattern of authority.

1) The gift of prophecy, familiar to students of the New Testament, continued to influence the thinking of second-century saints. Ignatius believes himself moved by the Spirit (*Phila.* 7), while the *Didache* and the *Shepherd of Hermas* give instructions for distinguishing the false prophet from the true. Apparently this problem was becoming increasingly acute. *Hermas* teaches that any man who claims to have the Spirit must be proved by "his life and his works." He who has the Spirit of God is "quiet and humble-minded, and refrains from all wickedness and the vain desire of this present world." But the pretender "exalts himself and desires to take the first place." He is "at once impudent, shameless and talkative, and surrounds himself with luxuries and many other deceits" (*Mand.* XI, 8,12). The *Didache* agrees. If a prophet can pass the test of character he merits the esteem of the church. Otherwise he is to be rejected.

This prophetic gift continued to appear in the church until Irenaeus' time (*A.H.* V,6,1), and some expected it to persist until the return of Christ (Eusebius, *H.E.* V,17). The movement called Montanism revived the early emphasis upon the gift in a dramatic way. It seems that Montanus, the founder of the sect in Asia Minor, would suddenly be seized by an ecstatic frenzy. He would rave and utter strange sounds. "I am the Lord God Almighty, dwelling in man," he would shout. "It is neither angel nor ambassador, but I, God the Father, who am come" (Epiphanius, *Refutation* XLVIII,11).

If such utterances were typical of the movement in its early stages, then it was guilty of fanaticism but not of profanity and blasphemy as its catholic opponents charged. Its greatest danger lay in sensationalism and in laying aside the written Word. Some Montanists professed that they had learned more from Montanus than from the Law and the Prophets or even from the Gospels. Others placed Maximilla and Priscilla, the two prophetesses who accompanied Montanus in his travels, above the apostles and Christ (Hippolytus, *Ref.* VIII,12).

Later advocates of the prophecy show considerably more restraint. Tertullian, the most famous convert, found Montanism attractive not because it offered any new teaching but because of the assurance that it seemed to give that the Holy Spirit was still the teacher of the church. He recognized that the movement itself was new but contended that the Spirit in the movement was not new:

> The Paraclete brings in nothing new. He does but state clearly what He has already hinted, and claims what He has kept in abeyance. . . . He should be regarded as the restorer rather than the originator (*Monog.* 3, 4).

The ministry of the Spirit as Tertullian conceived it lay primarily in behavior, not in doctrine:

> The Paraclete . . . will first bear witness to Christ Himself . . . and glorify Him and bring Him to our remembrance; and when thus recognized by His adherence to the fundamental rule of faith, He will proceed to reveal many things which appertain to the conduct of life (*Monog.* 2).

Development is thus in the sphere of ethics rather than in the sphere of dogma. "What," Tertullian asks, "does the dispensation of the Spirit mean but disciplinary guidance, the opening of the Scriptures, the remolding of the mind, and a general advance to better things?" (*Veiling of Virgins* 1).

Perhaps the most convincing proof that Tertullian did not look upon the ministry of the Spirit as an addition to the true faith rests in the fact that he brought no charge of heresy against his catholic opponents. He did not claim that Montanism added to catholic doctrine (*Against Praxeas* 8,13,30). On the contrary, he confessed that Montanus, Priscilla, and Maximilla challenged not a single article of the true faith (*On Fasting* 1).

Therefore, however the historian may interpret the early Christian claims to the Spirit-inspired gift of prophecy, it is clear that the early Christians themselves did not generally look upon this activity of the Spirit as in any sense supplanting his witness in the written Word.

2) The work of the Spirit in inspiring the biblical writers was so widely held in the early church as to demand no extensive treatment here. We have referred to this fact a number of times in the chapters of this study. Perhaps a summary statement will suffice at this point.

The Apostolic Fathers, while still living in the age of

ecstacy and prophecy, carry forward the apostolic idea of the inspiration of the Old Testament writers and begin to speak of the apostles as having been under the same influence of the Spirit. Barnabas considers the Spirit the teacher of the Old Testament saints. "Moses spake by the Spirit" or "David spake through the Spirit" are his customary introductions to Old Testament references. Clement's epistle is much the same, only in his work the apostles share the inspiration of the prophets (42:3,4). Paul in particular is singled out as under the influence of the Holy Spirit when he wrote to the Corinthians (47:3).

The same idea is expressed in the Apologists, except in their writings the Spirit is often confused with the pre-existent nature of the Logos. Theophilus' remark is typical: "the Logos, being the Spirit of God . . . came down on the prophets" (*Autol.* II,10). The fulfillment of Old Testament prophecies, argued the Apologists, proves that the prophets spoke under inspiration. They were, as Theophilus twice says, "Spirit-bearing men" (*Autol.* I,14). This gift of the Spirit the Gospel writers shared (*Autol.* II,9,22).

The Alexandrians perpetuate the same general view of inspiration. Clement speaks of those who fall from eminence when they do not follow God wherever he leads. "And He leads us in the inspired Scriptures" (*Misc.* VII,16). Origen adds that the Spirit who inspires the Scriptures also enables us to interpret them (*Epistle to Gregory* 3).

Thus the early Christian writers unitedly witness to the inspiration of the Scriptures by the Holy Spirit, the same Spirit who now lives in the church.

3) While the early Fathers do not give as much attention to the witness of the Spirit in the life of the believer as they do to his witness in Scripture, their comments are extremely important. From the earliest days of the sub-apostolic age there are passing references to this work of the Spirit, but as the century progresses the challenge of Monarchianism (the emphasis upon the unity of God) tended to focus more clearly upon the Spirit as the source of enlightenment. Later still the church came to be considered the depository of the Spirit. As early as Ignatius we find testimony to the work of the Spirit in all the faithful because it is the Spirit who

brings the soul into vital contact with the redemption provided by Christ (*Eph.* 9). Later this seminal thought springs up in Justin's writings. He had encountered the idea from his earliest contact with Christianity. His unnamed friend by the seashore laid great stress upon the inward testimony of the Spirit. When Justin quotes Plato to the effect that God can be apprehended only by the mind, the old man replies, "Is there then in our minds a power such as this and so great as this? Will the human mind ever see God unless it is furnished with the Holy Spirit?" (*Dial.* 4).

Then as the two are about to depart the elderly stranger urges Justin, "Pray that the gates of light may be opened to you; for these matters cannot be perceived or comprehended by any unless God and His Christ give power to understand" (*Dial.* 7). Apparently Justin did not forget these words, for he writes of baptism, "This bath is called 'illumination,' since those who learn these things have the mind illumined" (I *Apol.* 61).

The development of the doctrine of the Trinity resulting from Monarchian teaching added to this idea that the Holy Spirit is the internal witness. In his *Against Praxeas* Tertullian speaks of our being taught by the Paraclete who leads us into all truth (ch. 2). And Hippolytus writes in his treatise *Against Noetus*: "He who commands is the Father, He who obeys is the Son, He who gives understanding is the Holy Spirit." A bit later he adds, "What the Father wills, the Son translates into an act, and the Spirit manifests" (8-14). Thus the office of the Spirit is that of enabling the human understanding to grasp the revelation of the Father's will brought by the incarnate Son.

Toward the close of the second century and the beginning of the third this view of the Spirit's ministry continues to appear. For example, Clement of Alexandria writes: "The Lord . . . invites all men to come to the knowledge of the truth, and has sent the Paraclete for that end" (*Exhort.* IX, 85). And Origen explains how this work of the Spirit is fulfilled: "We pray that the light of the knowledge of the glory of God may shine in our hearts, the Spirit of God resting on our imaginations and enabling us to imagine the things of God" (*Against Celsus* IV, 95).

However, about this same time another idea concerning the Spirit receives special emphasis. Believers, especially in the West, begin to look upon the church as the home of the Spirit. Irenaeus says that true believers "have salvation written in their hearts without paper and ink by the Spirit" (*A.H.* III,4,2), but the individual receives the Holy Spirit only as he receives the truth preached in the church. "Where the church is, there is also the Spirit of God, and where the Spirit of God is, there is the church and every kind of grace; for the Spirit is truth" (*A.H.* IV,33,9). To reject the truth is thus to reject the Spirit. To reject the Spirit is to reject the church.

According to Novatian (d.257), the presence of the Spirit in the church marks the difference between this age and the age of the Prophets. In the Old Testament the Spirit was given to individuals and only occasionally. But in the New Testament He came to be in the church forever (*On the Trinity*, 29).

Thus the mission of the Holy Spirit was twofold: to inspire the biblical writers and to enlighten the believer. But there was one important difference in the two functions. "The faithful have the Spirit of God," writes Tertullian, "but the faithful are not the apostles. Apostles have the Holy Spirit in a special manner, in the fulness of His gifts and powers" (*Exhortation to Chastity* 4). In this way a place was reserved for the Spirit in the expanding life of the church, while the supremacy of the apostolic testimony continued unchallenged.

This brings us to a final word about a problem passage in Irenaeus' great work and its reputed support of the view that the Spirit especially endows those in the episcopal succession. Both Irenaeus and Tertullian, as we have seen, appeal to the succession lists of certain churches established by the apostles. The argument was used as a pledge of doctrinal unity and was based, as we have noted, on historical, not dogmatic, grounds.

In one passage, however, Irenaeus seems to add something to this historical conception of succession. He writes, "We ought to listen to the elders who are in the church, who have the succession from the apostles, those who, with the succession of the episcopate, have received the certain gift of truth [*charisma veritatis certum*] according to the good pleasure of the Father" (*A.H.* IV,26,2).

The problem in the passage turns on the meaning of *charisma veritatis*. Gregory Dix feels that Irenaeus' argument is "strikingly similar" to the view that Roman Catholics hold of "Papal Succession" to the chair of Peter in Rome. This view traces the succession from the contemporary Pope back to Peter through his predecessors, and not through the bishops who consecrate him to the episcopate, as Anglo-Catholics hold. The "charisma" is attached to the bishops *having become* bishop rather than to the *means by which* he became bishop, to the office itself rather than to the entrance upon the office.[2]

Dix, however, draws more from Irenaeus' passage than is there. The "charisma," rather than being a sacramentally mediated endowment of infallibility, is most likely the deposit of faith itself, the message of truth to which we must give attentive ears. It is significant that elders as well as bishops have received the "charisma" and that nothing is said about consecration and ordination. Irenaeus was too deeply convinced that the whole church is the sphere of the Spirit to entertain the notion that office-holders exclusively possessed the "charisma." Where the church is, he writes, there is the Spirit of God, and where the Spirit of God is, there is the church and every kind of grace; for the Spirit is truth.

[2] "The Ministry in the Early Church," in *The Apostolic Ministry*, ed. by Kenneth E. Kirk, pp. 209-210.

SELECTED BIBLIOGRAPHY

Original Sources and Translations

Baillie, J. and others (ed.). *The Library of Christian Classics.* Vols. I, II, and V. Philadelphia: Westminster, 1953.

Butterworth, G. W. (trans.). *Origen on First Principles.* London: S. P. C. K., 1936.

Dix, Gregory. *The Apostolic Tradition.* London: S. P. C. K., 1937.

Easton, Burton S. (trans.). *The Apostolic Tradition of Hippolytus.* London: Cambridge, 1934.

Grant, Robert M. *Gnosticism.* New York: Harper, 1961.

James, M. R. *The Apocryphal New Testament.* London: Oxford at the Clarendon, 1953.

Lake, K. (trans.). *The Apostolic Fathers.* 2 vols. Loeb Classical Library. London: Heinemann, 1952.

————, and Oulton, J. E. L. (trans.). *Eusebius: The Ecclesiastical History.* 2 vols. London: Heinemann, 1926-1932.

Lightfoot, J. B. *The Apostolic Fathers.* 5 vols. London: Macmillan, 1885-1890.

Migne, J. P. *Patrologiae Cursus Completus* (Series Graeca). 161 vols. Paris: 1857-1912.

Roberts, A., and Donaldson, J. (eds.). *Ante-Nicene Christian Library.* 10 vols. New York: Scribner's, 1926.

Books

Barth, Karl. *Church Dogmatics* I, 1 and 2. Trans. G. T. Thomson and Harold Knight. Edinburgh: T. & T. Clark, 1936, 1956.

Bethune-Baker, J. F. *An Introduction to Early History of Christian Doctrine.* 3rd ed. London: Methuen, 1923.
Blackman, E. C. *Marcion and His Influence.* London: S. P. C. K., 1948.
Brunner, Emil. *Revelation and Reason.* Trans. Olive Wyon. Philadelphia: Westminster, 1946.
Cross, F. L. *The Early Christian Fathers.* London: Gerald Duckworth & Co., 1960.
Cullmann, Oscar. *The Earliest Christian Confessions.* Trans. J. K. S. Ried. London: Lutterworth, 1949.
Dillistone, F. W., and others. *Scripture and Tradition.* London: Lutterworth, 1955.
Filson, Floyd V. *Which Books Belong in the Bible?* Philadelphia: Westminster, 1957.
Flesseman-Van Leer, E. *Tradition and Scripture in the Early Church.* Assen: Van Gorcum, 1954.
Forsyth, P. T. *The Principle of Authority.* London: Hodder and Stoughton, n.d.
Geldenhuys, J. Norval. *Supreme Authority.* Grand Rapids: Eerdmans, 1953.
Grant, R. M. *The Bible in the Church.* New York: Macmillan, 1948.
————. *Gnosticism and Early Christianity.* New York: Columbia Univ. Press, 1959.
————. *The Letter and the Spirit.* London: S. P. C. K., 1957.
Hanson, R. P. C. *Origen's Doctrine of Tradition.* London: S. P. C. K., 1954.
————. *Tradition in The Early Church.* London: S. C. M. Press, 1962.
Harnack, Adolph. *History of Dogma.* Vol. II of 5 vols. Trans. Neil Buchanan. Boston: Roberts Brothers, 1897.
————. *The Origin of the New Testament.* Trans. J. R. Wilkinson. London: Williams and Norgate, 1925.
Harris, R. Laird. *Inspiration and Canonicity.* Grand Rapids: Zondervan, 1957.
Headlam, A. C. *The Doctrine of the Church.* Bampton Lectures 1920. London: John Murray, 1923.
Kelly, J. N. D. *Early Christian Creeds.* London: Longmans, Green and Co., 1950.
————. *Early Christian Doctrines.* New York: Harper, 1958.
Knox, John. *Marcion and the New Testament.* Chicago: University of Chicago Press, 1942.
————. *The Early Church and the Coming Great Church.* New York: Abingdon, 1955.
Lawson, J. *The Biblical Theology of Saint Irenaeus.* London: Epworth, 1948.

Selected Bibliography 161

Lindsay, Thomas M. *The Church and the Ministry in the Early Church.* New York: Doran, n.d.
Manson, T. W. *The Church's Ministry.* London: Hodder & Stoughton, 1948.
Moffatt, James. *The Thrill of Tradition.* New York: Macmillan, 1944.
Paterson, W. P. *The Rule of Faith.* London: Hodder and Stoughton, 1912.
Prestige, G. L. *Fathers and Heretics.* London: S. P. C. K., 1948.
Ramm, Bernard. *The Pattern of Religious Authority.* Grand Rapids: Eerdmans, 1959.
Richardson, A., and Schweitzer, W. *Biblical Authority for Today.* Philadelphia: Westminster, 1951.
Sanday, William. *Inspiration.* Bampton Lectures 1893. 3rd ed. London: Longmans, 1896.
Schürer, Emil. *A History of the Jewish People at the Time of Jesus Christ.* 5 vols. Trans. J. Macpherson and others. Edinburgh: T. & T. Clark, 1885-1886.
Souter, Alexander. *The Text and Canon of the New Testament.* 2nd ed. revised by C. S. C. Williams. London: Duckworth, 1954.
Streeter, B. H. *The Primitive Church.* New York: Macmillan, 1929.
Swete, H. B. (ed.). *Essays on the History of the Church and the Ministry.* London: Macmillan, 1918.
―――. *The Holy Spirit in the Ancient Church.* London: Macmillan, 1912.
Torrance, T. F. *The Doctrine of Grace in the Apostolic Fathers.* Edinburgh: Oliver and Boyd, 1948.
Turner, H. E. W. *The Pattern of Christian Truth.* Bampton Lectures 1954. London: Mowbray, 1954.
Westcott, B. F., *General Survey of the History of the Canon of the New Testament.* London: Macmillan, 1896.
Williams, R. R. *Authority in the Apostolic Age.* London: S. C. M., 1950.

Articles

Bainvel, Jean. "Tradition," *The Catholic Encyclopedia,* XV, 6-13. New York: Robert Appleton, 1907-1914.
Berkowski, Stanislaus de Dunn. "Hierarchy of the Early Church," *The Catholic Encyclopedia,* VII, 326-344.
Cullmann, Oscar. "The Tradition," *The Early Church.* Ed. by A. J. B. Higgins. Philadelphia: Westminster, 1956.
Dix, Gregory. "The Ministry in the Early Church," *The Apostolic Ministry.* Ed. by Kenneth E. Kirk. London: Hodder & Stoughton, 1946.

Enslin, Morton S. "Irenaeus: Mostly Prolegomena," *Harvard Theological Review*, XL (1947), 137-165.

Farmer, Herbert H. "The Bible: Its Significance and Authority," *Interpreter's Bible*, I, 3-31, New York: Abingdon-Cokesbury, 1952.

Harnack, Adolph. "Apostolisches Symbolum," *Realencyklopädie für protestantische Theologie und Kirche*, I, 741-743. Leipzig: J. C. Hinrichs', 1897-1906.

Lietzmann, Hans. "Symbolstudien," *Zeitschrift für die Neutestamentliche Wissenschaft*, XXI (1922), 1-34; XXII (1923), 257-279; XXIV (1925), 193-202; XXVI (1927), 75-95.

Lightfoot, J. B. "The Christian Ministry," *Saint Paul's Epistle to the Philippians*, 8th ed., 181-269. London: Macmillan, 1885.

Molland, E. "Irenaeus of Lugdunum and Apostolic Succession," *Journal of Ecclesiastical History*, I (1950), 12-28.

Piana, George La. "The Roman Church at the End of the Second Century," *Harvard Theological Review*, XVIII (July, 1925), 201-271.

Prestige, G. L. "Tradition," *Theology*, XIII (July, 1926), 8-14.

Reid, George J. "Canon of the Holy Scriptures," *The Catholic Encyclopedia*, III, 267-279.

Ridderbos, Herman. "The Canon of the New Testament," *Revelation and the Bible*. Ed. by Carl F. H. Henry. Grand Rapids: Baker, 1958.

Strack, H. L. and Zahn, T. "Canon of Scripture," *New Schaff-Herzog Encyclopedia*, II, 388-400. Grand Rapids: Baker, 1951-1954.

Van Hove, A. "Hierarchy," *The Catholic Encyclopedia*, VII, 322-326.

INDEX OF NAMES

Aristides, 61-63
Athanasius, 22, 114
Athenagoras, 76-78, 81, 118

Barry, G. D., 26
Barth, Karl, 14, 148
Basilides, 113, 126

Celsus, 11
Clement of Alexandria, 46, 49, 126-138, 155, 156
Clement of Rome, 30-35, 39-40, 56, 57, 58, 59, 155
Cross, F. L., 26
Cullmann, Oscar, 18, 146
Cyprian, 20, 23, 91
Cyril of Jerusalem, 94, 110

D'Espine, Henri, 14
Dionysius of Alexandria, 82, 91
Dix, Gregory, 158
Domitian, 30

Eddy, Mary Baker, 150
Eusebius, 15, 35, 53, 61, 78, 82, 90, 110, 114, 126

Flesseman-Van Leer, E., 29, 43, 44, 77, 104
Forsyth, P. T., 149

Grant, Robert M., 48, 119

Hadrian, 61
Hanson, R. P. C., 130
Harnack, Adolf, 15, 16, 85
Harris, J. Rendel, 61, 63
Headlam, A. C., 145
Hegesippus, 110, 145
Hippolytus, 88-89, 91, 156

Ignatius, 16, 35-40, 56, 59, 90, 153, 155
Irenaeus, 19, 30, 41, 44, 84-125, 137-138, 144, 145, 147, 153, 157, 158

Jerome, 147
Justin, 56, 63-72, 81, 82, 91, 92, 100, 112, 113, 116, 144, 156

Kattenbusch, F., 110
Kaye, John, 65, 66
Kelly, J. N. D., 19, 44, 50, 58, 63, 70, 110, 111
Kleist, James A., 30-31

Lebreton, Jules, 80
Leonides, 127
LeSaint, W. P., 119
Lietzmann, Hans, 89, 92
Lightfoot, J. B., 33, 44, 46
Lucks, Henry A., 77

Marcellus of Ancyra, 88, 89, 94

Marcion, 22, 44, 55, 56, 82, 84, 85,
  102, 120, 121
Marcus, 93
Marcus Aurelius, 76
Maximilla & Priscilla, 153, 154
Minucius Felix, 80
Moffat, James, 102
Montanus, 153, 154

Newman, John Henry, 147
Novatian, 157

Octavius, 80
Origen, 46, 127-138, 144, 155, 156

Pantaenus, 126, 127
Papias, 21, 53-54, 57, 114
Philo, 102, 132, 136
Pius, Antonius, 64
Pius, Bishop of Rome, 49
Plato, 101, 156
Polycarp, 36, 41-46, 55, 57, 58, 85,
  86, 105
Ponthinus, Bishop of Lyons, 86
Prestige, G. L., 132, 149

Quadratus, 61

Radford, L. B., 76
Richardson, Alan, 15
Robinson, J. A., 30, 62
Rufinus of Aquileia, 87, 110

Schaff, Philip, 85
Schürer, E., 101
Schweitzer, Wolfgang, 15
Serapion, Bishop of Antioch, 15
Soter, Bishop of Rome, 82

Tatian, 72-73, 113
Tertullian, 16, 19, 20, 44, 84-125,
  137, 144, 145, 147, 153-154, 156,
  157
Theophilus, 78-80, 81, 82, 155
Torrance, T. F., 28, 40
Trajan, 36
Trypho, the Jew, 64, 65, 69
Turner, C. H., 18, 35, 36, 39
Turner, H. E. W., 16, 116

Valentinus, 113, 121, 126
Valla, Lorenzo, 88

Westcott, B. F., 26, 31, 43, 65, 66
Williams, B. B., 56

INDEX OF SUBJECTS

Apocrypha, 52, 58, 115, 146
apostles, 15, 25, 27, 36, 41-42, 49, 64, 65-66, 74-75, 77, 149, 157
authority,
  apostolic, 15, 16-17, 36, 57-58
  Orthodoxy, 12-13, 17
  Protestant, 13, 18, 140-141, 148
  Roman Catholic, 12, 17, 141-142, 146

Barlaam & Josaphat, Lives of, 62
Barnabas, 46-49, 56, 132, 135, 155
Bishop, 158
  in Clement, 34-35
  in Ignatius, 39-40
  in Hermas, 51
  in Clement (Alex.), 131

canon, 22-24, 111-112, 141, 146
  in Clement (Alex.), 131, 132, 134-135
  in Irenaeus & Tertullian, 116-117
  in Origen, 134-135
  Marcionite, 113
  Muratorian, 113
  tests of 114-116, 143, 144
charisma, 29, 30, 158
charters, the, 38-39
Clement II, 51-53, 59, 115
councils,
  Nicea, 17, 18, 90

Trent, 141, 146
Vatican (1870), 141, 146
Creed, Apostles', 18, 87-95
creed, 17, 18, 19, 34, 36, 45, 50, 58, 63, 70, 91, 93-94, 128-129
custom, 20, 102

Didache, 26-30, 51, 114-115, 135, 153

ecumenism, 14
Edinburgh, I.M.C., 14
Eldad & Modat, Book of, 50
episcopacy, 34, 39, 106
Exhortation to the Greeks, 71

Gnosticism, 23, 55, 85, 87, 93, 96, 102, 103, 120, 121, 126, 128, 136-137, 150
  Christian, 130, 133, 134
gnosis, 48, 49, 56
gospel, 37, 38, 62, 65, 97, 148
Gospels, 28, 37, 53, 54, 65-66, 75, 77, 112, 146
grace, 35, 68, 75-76

Hermas, Shepherd of, 49-51, 56, 115, 135, 153
Holy Spirit, 12, 29-30, 32-33, 51, 61, 63, 66, 67, 79, 107, 118, 119, 136, 140, 152-158

infallibility, papal, 17-18

inspiration, 47, 51, 54, 66-67, 73, 77-78, 79, 81, 118-119, 135-136
interpretation of Scripture, 67-68, 119-124, 132, 136-137, 141, 147

Letter of the Apostles, 92, 93
Letter to Diognetus, 73-76, 82
liberalism, 13-14, 142
logia, 32, 44
logos, 64, 66, 67, 74

Martyrdom of Polycarp, 45-46
ministry, 59, 140, 148
Monarchianism, 93, 124, 155, 156
Muratorian Fragment, 116, 118

Neo-Orthodoxy, 14

rule of faith, 19-20
  in Apologists, 82, 89
  in Clement (Alex.), 131-132
  in Irenaeus, 95-97, 131
  in Justin, 69-70
  in Origen, 132-133, 144
  in Polycarp, 43-44, 58
  in Tertullian, 97-99, 131

Scripture, 140, 149
  in Apologists, 81-83
  in Aristides, 62-63
  in Athenagoras, 76-77
  in *Barnabas*, 46-48

  in Clement (Alex.), 133-134
  in Clement (Rome), 31-33
  in *II Clement*, 52-53
  in *Didache*, 28-29
  in *Hermas*, 50-51
  in Ignatius, 37-39
  in Justin, 64
  in *Letter to Diognetus*, 75
  in Origen, 133-134
  in Polycarp, 42-43
  in Tatian, 72-73
  in Theophilus, 78
succession, 35, 40, 42, 70, 104-106, 108-110, 131, 145, 158

theology, 12
tradition, 13, 20-21, 35, 57, 58, 65 66, 69, 71, 100-103, 107, 110-111, 131-132, 141-144, 150
  in Clement (Alex.), 129-130
  in Clement (Rome), 33-34
  in Diognetus, 75
  in Ireneaus, 102-104
  in Justin, 68-69
  in Origen, 130
  in Papias, 53-54
  in Tertullian, 106-108
Trinity, 68, 91, 92, 156, 157

World Council of Churches, 14